VERSION 2

Mass Media and Popular Culture

Barry Duncan

Janine D'Ippolito

Cam Macpherson

Carolyn Wilson

HARCOURT
BRACE
CANADA

Harcourt Brace & Company, Canada

Canadian Cataloguing in Publication Data

Main entry under title:
Mass media and popular culture
Version 2.

Includes index.
ISBN 0-7747-0170-6

1. Mass media. 2. Popular culture. I. Duncan, Barry, 1936-

P91.D86 1996 302.23 C96-930607-5

The authors and publisher gratefully acknowledge the following educators for their evaluations and suggestions:
Dan Blake, Teacher, North Surrey Secondary School, Surrey, **British Columbia**
Bob Pace, Teacher, Robert Usher Collegiate, Regina, **Saskatchewan**
John Pungente, SJ, Director, Jesuit Communication Project, Toronto, **Ontario**
Barbara Rager, Teacher, Canterbury High School, Ottawa, **Ontario**
Mary Wentz, Teacher, Sir Sandford Fleming High School, North York, **Ontario**
Eileen O'Connell, Teacher, Cornwallis Junior High School, Halifax, **Nova Scotia**

This has been an inspiring project aided by understanding editors and supported by family, friends, and media literacy colleagues, especially those whose lives have crossed ours through the Association for Media Literacy. Equally important have been our media students, who keep us honest and remind us why popular culture is so important and so popular.

—Barry Duncan, Janine D'Ippolito, Cam Macpherson, and Carolyn Wilson

Project Manager: Lydia Fletcher
Project Editors: Donna Adams, Marie Verdun
Editorial Manager: Nicola Balfour
Senior Production Editor: Margot Miller
Manager of Art and Design: Dennis Boyes
Production Manager: Sue-Ann Becker
Production Coordinators: Donna Dowsett/Sheila Barry
Text Design and Layout: Sharon Foster Design
Permissions Editor: Mary Rose MacLachlan
Photo Researcher: Laura Edlund
Cover Design: Sharon Foster Design
Cover Illustration: Paul Watson

∞ Printed in Canada on acid-free paper

1 2 3 4 5   00 99 98 97 96

Contents

This book is part of a media literacy program that includes this textbook, an accompanying Resource Binder, and a video package entitled *Scanning Television: Videos for Media Literacy in Class.*

    Throughout this text you will find icons which refer you to related information in the text and to the other program components.

Points you to
text references.

Points you to
Resource Binder
references.

Points you to
video package
references.

Contents by Medium

CHAPTER 1

What Are the Mass Media and Popular Culture?

We live in a media-filled and information-rich culture. By the time you finish high school, you will have spent an average of 11 000 hours in school and 15 000 hours watching television. Add to that the time spent watching films, reading magazines and newspapers, surfing the Internet, listening to music, and looking at advertising, and the result is many, many hours of media involvement. The purpose of this book is to help you develop a critical perspective on the media and popular culture.

Mass Media and Popular Culture, Version 2 asks you to examine critically some of the most important media issues of our time—from concerns of global importance such as who owns and who has access to the media, to the personal significance of shopping malls and music; from how to interpret media images of nationality, gender, and race, to the impact of new and converging communications and entertainment technologies.

While examining these issues, you will also be asked to explore the nature and influence of the traditional communications media—film, television, music, and popular print.

Why the Mass Media Are Important

Today, the fastest-growing areas of the work force are the information, education, and knowledge sectors. These sectors are responsible for producing huge quantities of information plus the technology needed to access it. They have created the "information highway" by merging new and evolving communications technologies such as the Internet and high-tech computers. This highway enables us to travel the world electronically and it may dramatically change our lives, from where and how we work to what we do in our leisure time. These technologies have made possible a new frontier—cyberspace—and have given us the means to explore it.

Perhaps of even greater significance is the fact that our society tells its stories through the media. Music, film, and television help us to understand who we are and what is happening in our world. In order to participate fully in our information society, we need to be media literate. That is, we must understand the impact of the mass media on our daily lives.

mass media: the methods of communication used to reach large numbers of people at the same time—TV, newspapers, radio, magazines, films, books, the Internet

Here are six of the key roles the mass media play in our lives.

1. The media supply information about important events both at home and on the other side of the world. Without the media to keep us informed, we would know little about what happens outside our daily lives.

2. The media influence what we talk and think about, whether it's the latest hit movie, a celebrity scandal, Canadian politics, or a medical breakthrough. Our knowledge and opinions are shaped by the information and viewpoints the media provide.

Seventy percent of North Americans learn about world events from television news.

3. The media allow us to expand our personal experience. They allow us to share in adventures like an African safari or to witness the horrors of war or famine.

4. The media show us the images we come to accept as normal. Media personalities, models, and performers set standards of appearance, language, and behaviour that influence us all.

5. Advertising and public relations messages reach us through the media, persuading us to buy products, accept ideas, and adopt positive images of institutions and corporations.

6. The media entertain us. We spend much of our leisure time listening to radio and CDs or watching TV and movies.

Activity

1. Find examples of mass media products (for example, newspaper articles, TV shows, films, music videos, posters) that play each of the six key roles mentioned above, and be prepared to explain how they play these roles. Include examples from recent national and international news.

Characteristics of Popular Culture

Popular culture includes Barbie and Ken dolls, fashion fads, gossip about pop stars, the local shopping mall, video games, TV sitcoms, summer blockbuster movies, and souvenirs from rock concerts. Popular culture also includes the active ways we include popular culture products and experiences in our daily lives. When we display posters of actors or sports stars in our bedrooms or lockers, collect ticket stubs from rock concerts, exchange gossip with friends about movies, TV shows, and rock bands, and surf the Internet, we are actively involved with popular culture.

"In the simplest terms, popular culture is best thought of as mainstream culture—the arts, artifacts, entertainments, fads, beliefs and values shared by large segments of the society."
—*The Popular Culture Reader,* 1983

▲ *Murphy Brown*

See Video 1, Excerpt 3.

▲ *The Simpsons*

▲ *North of 60*

Popular culture tries to appeal to as large an audience as possible, so it tends to preserve the "status quo," rarely challenging currently accepted values. Views on social trends, the role of women, minority groups, and definitions of happiness—all are influenced by the dominant social, political, and economic system. A careful analysis of popular culture will reveal the beliefs or myths that communicate the desires, fears, and hopes of dominant North American culture.

Many important social issues are dramatized in the media. The media profoundly influence our concepts of justice, our trust in the law, our understanding of the plight of battered women, our response to sexual harassment, and our attitudes towards race relations. High-profile trials such as those of Paul Bernardo or O. J. Simpson, prompt personal reflection and discussion about appropriate behaviour and society's moral code. Television programs such as *Murphy Brown*, *Roseanne*, and *The Simpsons* have become a kind of testing ground for exploring controversial topics, such as single parenthood, lesbian and gay relationships, and public concern about excessive violence in the media.

By examining the patterns, values, and ideologies in popular culture, we can take the pulse of society. For example, if you listen to some of the pop songs of the 1960s or 1970s, watch television reruns of *Happy Days* or *All in the Family*, or browse through back issues of magazines such as *Life* and *Maclean's*, you will discover the social trends and concerns of those times. You should remember, however, that although those media products can give you a broad picture of the times, they may not give a true reflection of society—not all families are like the Cunninghams or the Bunkers.

Activities

1. In your media log, write a list of all your encounters with popular culture over two days. Include radio and TV shows, movies, billboards, music, magazines, observations about fads, fashion, and hairstyles, current slang, and visits to shopping malls. Share your list with other students. What did you learn about the nature of popular culture through this exercise? (For more on Media Logs, see page 5.)

2. "Rollerblades and Barbie dolls, *Roseanne* and *Seinfeld*, baseball caps and baggy pants...." Working in groups, add as many pairs as you can to this list of current popular culture products. Choose ten examples from your list and explain how each one communicates the desires, fears, and hopes of our culture. For example, a Barbie doll shows us one popular fantasy of how women should look and dress.

3. List the names of people who have had extensive coverage in the media in recent years, for example, Lucien Bouchard, k.d. lang, O.J. Simpson, Silken Laumann. What social or cultural issues were these people associated with? Describe how popular culture treated one of the people on your list by looking at how they were dealt with on talk shows or in dramatized reenactments on TV, and in jokes and magazine articles.

> **Media Log**
>
> Keep a separate notebook for recording your personal responses to the mass media and popular culture, and your opinions about related issues. Typical entries in this media log might include
>
> - your thoughts and observations on the coverage of a media event, an ongoing news story, or a popular culture trend
> - your views on a controversial media topic, for example, censorship, or the use of stereotypes
> - your evaluation of class activities and any thoughts those activities raised
> - ideas and outlines for media projects, from making a video to writing an essay

Canadian and American Popular Culture

The mass media have played an important role in the development of Canada. Our country consists of a narrow band of settlements stretched from coast to coast across a vast continent. Finding ways to connect these settlements has formed a large part of our history. Sharing a border with a powerful and densely populated neighbour has also influenced our development. Many government reports have argued that our Canadian cultural identity would be completely overwhelmed by American programming if significant Canadian media content were not available. For this reason, the National Film Board and Canadian Broadcasting Corporation were created to develop and maintain our unique identity. We now have government regulations stating how much air time must be devoted to Canadian programming.

Canadians do indeed have a thriving popular culture to celebrate. Many of our best musicians, from Neil Young and Céline Dion to the Crash Test Dummies and Alanis Morissette, are well known far beyond our borders. The Canadian music industry is thriving as people, young and not so young, attend concerts and buy Canadian tapes and CDs.

Canadian filmmakers such as Norman Jewison have built successful Hollywood careers. At home in Canada, independent filmmakers such as Patricia Rozema, Robert Lepage, Atom Egoyan, and Denys Arcand have produced films that tell Canadian stories with universal appeal. Canadian television programs such as *Due South*, *SCTV*, *DeGrassi High*, *Road to Avonlea*, and *North of 60* have helped to build our sense of Canadian identity. They have also earned international sales for Canadian television programming.

▲ Canadian popular culture includes TV shows like
▼ *Due South* and sports teams like the Blue Jays.

TORONTO BLUE JAYS
BASEBALL CLUB

Many of Canada's best sports figures have won international acclaim and many Canadians love to watch our Olympic athletes, figure skaters, and hockey, football, and baseball teams on television. Toronto and Vancouver now have their own NBA franchise teams, the Raptors and the Grizzlies. When the Toronto Blue Jays won the World Series two years in a row in 1992 and 1993, Canadians were united from coast to coast in celebration. But Canadian commentators pointed out the irony that most of the "Canadian" players were drawn from the United States and Puerto Rico, demonstrating that popular culture has little regard for national borders.

See also
page 147.

Activity

See also
page 35.

1. In groups, brainstorm a list of images that represent Canadian popular culture. Include Canadian TV and radio programs, celebrities, sports figures, historical figures, literature, and even the items sold in souvenir shops. Did you notice any Canadian stereotypes? If so, how accurately do these stereotypes represent Canada and Canadians? What conclusions can you make about the characteristics of Canadian popular culture?

How the Media Construct Reality

Y ou are watching the news or a public affairs show on television. The pictures and the sound track seem very real; you are expected to believe what you see and hear, and accept the announcer or narrator as an authority on the events he or she describes. This is your "window on the world." Or is it?

Most television news favours the visual; producers like to show film footage of war scenes, terrorism, fires, auto accidents, riots, and strikes. Events that were left out of the newscast, such as a drop in the number of welfare cases in your community, could be as important as what was shown. As for public affairs shows, the producers may use only a small part of the video footage shot by the camera crew. A 20:1 ratio of footage shot to footage used is not unusual. How do producers decide what footage to use?

Producers create or "construct" media products—whether it's the 6 o'clock news, a TV drama, your daily newspaper, a magazine ad, or a CD—to make a world that is exciting and entertaining enough to keep audiences interested. Many choices and decisions are involved in the making of a media product. Producers must constantly ask themselves, What content will have the most audience appeal? What material looks best? How should a person, object, animal, or event be presented? What will grab—and hold—the audience's attention? The results may be far removed from reality.

Throughout this book you will investigate a variety of media products, or "texts," to determine the ways in which they are "constructed." In media studies, "text" refers to any form of reproduced communication, including books, magazines, films, television programs, CDs, advertisements, toys, and T-shirts. As a media student, you will "deconstruct" media texts to see how they were constructed and why, and to determine their effect on audiences.

media text: *any form of reproduced communication, from a book, film, or CD, to an ad, a toy, or a T-shirt*

deconstruct: *to take apart, analyze, or break down a media text into its component parts in order to understand how and why it was created*

The Media Triangle below provides you with a checklist of questions for deconstructing media texts. The triangle starts from the assumption that each media text is produced in a particular way, for a particular audience.

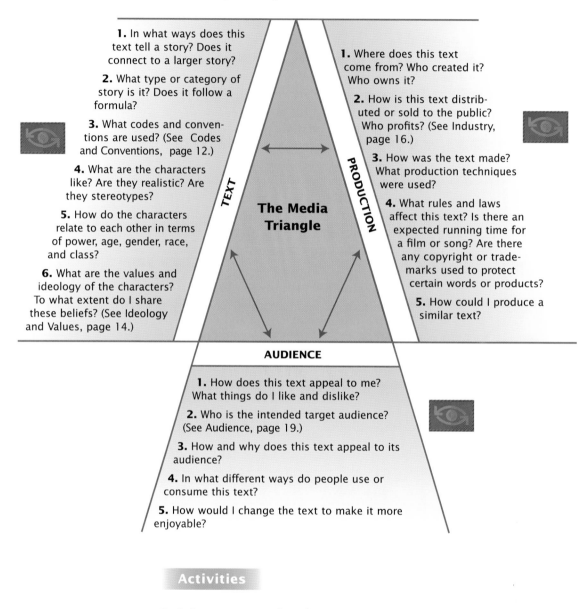

TEXT

1. In what ways does this text tell a story? Does it connect to a larger story?

2. What type or category of story is it? Does it follow a formula?

3. What codes and conventions are used? (See Codes and Conventions, page 12.)

4. What are the characters like? Are they realistic? Are they stereotypes?

5. How do the characters relate to each other in terms of power, age, gender, race, and class?

6. What are the values and ideology of the characters? To what extent do I share these beliefs? (See Ideology and Values, page 14.)

The Media Triangle

PRODUCTION

1. Where does this text come from? Who created it? Who owns it?

2. How is this text distributed or sold to the public? Who profits? (See Industry, page 16.)

3. How was the text made? What production techniques were used?

4. What rules and laws affect this text? Is there an expected running time for a film or song? Are there any copyright or trademarks used to protect certain words or products?

5. How could I produce a similar text?

AUDIENCE

1. How does this text appeal to me? What things do I like and dislike?

2. Who is the intended target audience? (See Audience, page 19.)

3. How and why does this text appeal to its audience?

4. In what different ways do people use or consume this text?

5. How would I change the text to make it more enjoyable?

Activities

1. Select a variety of media texts such as magazine ads, TV sitcoms, and movies, and use the Media Triangle to analyze how meaning is constructed in each one. For example, most tourism ads show an idealized vision of travel, and sitcoms show idealized, middle-class North American homes. What do these media texts say about living a "good life" and finding happiness?

2. **a)** In small groups, audio- or videotape an election interview. Have one person in the group play the role of a candidate for student council president while the others act as reporters interviewing the candidate. Each group member should then write one of the following stories about the interview: a positive story, a negative story, or a balanced story—giving both positive and negative information. As a group, read and compare the different stories.

b) Media critics say that reporters can never be truly objective, but they can be fair. Explain the difference between "being objective" and "being fair," making reference to your experience doing the previous assignment.

See also
page 155.

The Medium Is the Message

In the media, the storyline and content are not the only things that create meaning in a text. The form of each medium also affects the meaning. For example, television may stress the visual aspect of the story, radio may favour live interviews and commentary, while newspapers may provide more detailed background information, longer interviews, and photographs. Because of each medium's unique characteristics, there will be inevitable differences among them, even when the media are telling the same story.

A televised U.S. presidential debate between Richard Nixon and John F. Kennedy in 1960 illustrates the difference between radio and television. Those who heard the debate on radio believed Nixon had won, while the television audience believed the opposite. Nixon presented his arguments well, but he was sweating profusely and appeared uncomfortable, while Kennedy was cool and assured. The radio audience could not see what the men looked like, and so, to them, Nixon seemed to win. More people watched the debate than listened to it on radio, and Kennedy won the election.

Canadian communications expert Marshall McLuhan observed that each medium has its own unique rules or its own bias. Because of the built-in bias of each medium, the nature of the message delivered differs in each medium we encounter. For example, the lead story on the 6 o'clock TV news might be about a disastrous flood because it has eye-catching visuals; the lead story on radio might be about the Canadian economy because it has an excellent sound bite from a controversial politician. Reading a story is a completely different experience from listening to it on the radio or watching a version of it on TV. We must therefore pay attention to both the content of the message and the medium through which it is delivered. McLuhan expressed this idea in his memorable slogan, "The medium is the message."

Activity

1. Consider the following: The government is planning new legislation that will decrease support for the unemployed. A member of Parliament has just made a speech to justify the government's position. A large group of unemployed young people are present to protest and a struggle breaks out between the protesters and the police. Predict how this event will be covered by a newspaper, a radio station, and a television station. How do you think the coverage will differ and why? How much of this difference would be based on the characteristics unique to each medium?

Converging Media

Thirty years ago, each medium was clearly different from the others and they all competed with each other for our time and money. The films we enjoyed in theatres were nothing like the shows we watched at home on the small television screen. Each medium also affected us in different ways. For example, the telephone changed us from being letter-writers to talkers.

Today's new technologies have merged or blended the media so that we can barely tell where one ends and another begins. With fax machines, we can use telephone technology to send a written letter the same way we send our voices. We watch more movies at home than at theatres, thanks to video and cable television. Music videos with their visual images are now an essential part of the music industry.

In order to succeed in today's global economy, many large media companies have bought out or merged with their competitors. Now most of the world's film, television, and music production is controlled by a handful of multinational corporations. A single company, such as The Walt Disney Company, can make and distribute a feature film and its video, produce and market the film's sound track, develop a children's cartoon program based on the film, and broadcast the cartoon on the company's own television network.

With our home computers and CD-ROMs, we can combine printed text, graphics, and sound simultaneously. Today's computers communicate with both telephone and television systems through cable and satellite technology. Through the Internet, we gain access to a world-wide source of print, sound, and visual information and entertainment.

See also Video 4, Excerpt 38.

We can no longer think about or study a separate medium in isolation. We must study the media as rapidly changing components of global communications systems.

Activity

1. **a)** Imagine that you and a partner work for a large media corporation that has just acquired the rights to the best-selling novel, *The Hero's Last Revenge*. Prepare a plan to show how your corporation could adapt the novel for all of the different types of media they control. Real-life examples such as *Jurassic Park* and *Batman* have taken advantage of feature films, sound tracks, cartoons, video games, and merchandise such as action toys, lunch boxes, and T-shirts.
   b) How would you use the media and popular culture, such as fast-food outlets, to promote each of your media products?

Key Concepts of Mass Media and Popular Culture

The principles or concepts discussed on the following pages will provide a framework for your examination of mass media and popular culture.

Codes and Conventions

Codes and conventions are the familiar and predictable forms and techniques used by the media to communicate certain ideas or to convey a desired impression. For example, a TV news anchor usually sits behind a news desk and looks directly at the camera while reading the news, thereby creating an impression of authority. Or a horror film's dark, deserted settings and threatening music warn the viewer of coming disaster.

Normally, we understand these codes without being conscious of them. Technical codes include camera angles, sound, and lighting. Symbolic codes include the language, dress, and actions of characters, such as using a clenched fist to portray anger. Part of being media literate is being aware of these techniques and recognizing the effects they are meant to have.

Answer the following questions to help you identify some of the codes and conventions used by the media:

- In a television show, the camera moves in for a close-up of a man and woman. The lighting is dim and the music is soft and slow. What do think the scene is about?

- In movies such as the *Star Wars* trilogy or action hero films, how can you tell the bad guys from the good guys?

- What is the usual setting for family sitcoms on TV?

- In the popular music industry, how can you distinguish a heavy metal fan from a fan of alternative music?

- According to a recent ad campaign, what type of person drinks milk?

Activity

1. In groups, list some codes and conventions that are used in the following media texts: soap operas, horror films, rap music, heavy metal albums or CD covers, toys for girls, and toys for boys. Compare your list with that of another group.

Film Genres

One example of the use of codes and conventions can be found in the familiar formulas used to create a wide variety of feature films. Most of us have favourite types of films that we enjoy watching more than others. Some people love horror films, while others prefer comedies. These film types are called "genres." A genre is a category or form of film in which the subject matter, theme, and techniques are similar to other films of the same type. We recognize a genre because the characters, stories, and situations are familiar. Most films fit a particular genre or formula so that audiences know in advance what to expect. Below is a list of several popular genres.

Family Films: The story will focus on the relationships and conflicts in a family, but will avoid serious violence and strong language. *Mrs. Doubtfire* (1993); *Honey I Shrunk the Kids* (1989)

Science Fiction Films: These films will often be set in the future and will include conflict with strange, alien creatures and plenty of special effects. *2001: A Space Odyssey* (1968); *Star Wars* (1977)

Horror Films: Thrillers are often about ordinary people caught up in extraordinary events. Films that frighten the audience are so popular that filmmakers have produced many sub-genres, or specialized forms of horror films, such as "monster" films, or films about insane murderers or the supernatural. *Frankenstein* (1931); *Silence of the Lambs* (1990)

Westerns: These usually depict a conflict between good and evil in the "wild" west, and feature simple, stock characters, sweeping landscapes, frontier towns, and gunfights. *High Noon* (1952); *A Fistful of Dollars* (1964)

Disney: These are often animated films about good characters fighting against evil forces, always with a happy ending. *Snow White and the Seven Dwarfs* (1937); *The Lion King* (1994)

This list is by no means all-inclusive, as there are many other genres and sub-genres. Inventive filmmakers also create new genres, or genre busters, by making films that do not follow the

▲ *Mrs. Doubtfire*

▲ *Star Wars*

▲ *Frankenstein*

© Disney Enterprises, Inc.

▲ *The Lion King*

▲ Which elements in each of these stills identify the genre of the film?

expectations of a familiar genre or that combine the elements of more than one genre. For example, *Pulp Fiction* (1994) is both an absurd comedy and a thriller, but defies the expectations of both genres, and the *Aliens* series combines elements of both science fiction and horror films.

1. Five genres are described above. With a partner, discuss other types of films you enjoy and add at least three more genres to the list. Where possible, identify two or more sub-genres within the larger category and list the main characteristics of each.

2. a) Identify your favourite genre and describe its common elements. For example, what kinds of characters appear in these films, what kind of action takes place, where does the action take place, and what kind of endings do the films have?
b) Create a parody or humorous imitation of your chosen genre. Write a short script including several of the elements you have described, then perform or videotape the script.

Ideology and Values

We each have a set of beliefs about the world. These beliefs shape our fears, hopes, and desires, as well as our views on issues such as the roles of men and women, discipline in schools, and the importance of authority figures such as government leaders, police, and teachers. We use our own set of beliefs to define happiness, success, and morality. The term for this set of beliefs is "ideology."

Individual groups of people have unique ideologies. For example, a church group will have a very different set of beliefs from a gang of bikers. The people who produce, own, and control the media also have their own ideologies. Many of these people are middle- or upper-class men. What kind of messages do we receive through the media from this "dominant group"?

When we receive a message from the media, we interpret it through our personal ideology and values. If our interpretation of the message agrees with the dominant view, this is called a "preferred reading." It is important to note that "preferred" in this sense does not mean "better." If our interpretation disagrees with the dominant view, this is called an "oppositional reading." For example, a newspaper photo of a scuffle between striking workers and management could be read in these ways: the dominant, or preferred, reading might be that the fight is typical of strikers, that they are greedy troublemakers, and that the strike is unnecessary. An oppositional reading might be that management provoked the scuffle to make the strikers look bad and to win public opposition to the strikers and their legitimate concerns.

Some messages sent by the media are almost invisible—we are so used to the conventions that we may not be aware of any message. For example, in advertising, cars are often associated with beautiful women; beer is associated with a "party-time" lifestyle; and more women than men are concerned with clean clothes and sparkling dishes. Are these accurate representations? Do you agree with the values suggested by such commercials? How do American viewpoints affect Canadian values? Recognizing these invisible messages and the values they promote is part of being media literate. The Checklist for Ideology and Values below will help you analyze the ideology and values in any media text.

Activities

1. In a group, view two or three media texts, such as a TV show, a film, a music video, a video game, or some magazine ads. Use the Checklist for Ideology and Values to help you interpret their ideological messages. What social issues are dealt with? How might those ideological messages change if people of a different social class or race were included, or if the male and female characters switched roles?

2. Give a "preferred" and an "oppositional" reading of at least two of the following media texts: a soap opera, a Hollywood movie, a popular TV show, a lifestyle ad, or stories about a celebrity. Remember that the oppositional reading will differ from the interpretation of the producer and most of the audience.

Checklist for Ideology and Values

1. Does the text present the beliefs of one particular group?

2. Who is in a position of power? Who is not?

3. Does the text exclude any groups of people or their beliefs?

4. What stereotypes, if any, are used? To what effect?

5. What definitions of happiness, success, or morality are implied?

Industry

Many people believe that the media are there only to entertain and inform us, and that easy access to the media is simply one of the privileges of life in a technological society. But it is not that simple. The media and popular culture industries are a powerful and vast network of businesses made up of multi-billion dollar corporations that employ thousands of people, from the concert performers to the sound track recorders, the T-shirt and CD manufacturers, and the janitors who clean up after the show.

The companies creating and managing most of our entertainment and mass communications systems are owned by a small number of global giants such as Time Warner and The Walt Disney Company, both based in the United States. Since the 1980s, mergers among media companies in Canada, the United States, and other industrialized countries have created a concentration of ownership. If this trend continues, it has been predicted that by the year 2000, ninety percent of the world's information—books, magazines, newspapers, films, television programs, music, computer software, and data bases—will be owned by ten global corporations. Critics worry that this kind of control will influence how we tell our stories, what stories get told, and how we are represented.

Media mergers may limit our access to dissenting opinions. For example, a newspaper that is owned by the same company or person who owns the local television station may be reluctant to criticize that station's programs or sponsors. While we may seem to have more media choices in a 500-channel universe, there are really fewer voices because a small group of companies own most of the channels. This means that our sources of information about culture, governments, and society in general will be controlled by that small group of companies. The result may be a frightening kind of cultural homogenization, where all the news, TV shows, and movies will begin to look the same.

Canadian media are caught in this same global pattern. Although we have had regulations guaranteeing Canadian content, recent free trade agreements have lessened these protections. Canadian media companies could be bought up by global conglomerates and there is real concern that we could lose our own voice.

Media Facts

The following facts will help you realize the extent to which the media are "big business." They also show the relationships among the various members and branches of the media.

- The Walt Disney Company is now the world's largest entertainment corporation, owning amusement parks, a consumer products division, a publishing company, a television network, video production and distribution companies, two educational divisions, The Disney Channel, a music division, a production company for television and movies, a travel company, hotels, a TV station, and Capital Cities/ ABC Inc., which in turn owns television and radio stations, magazines, books, and newspapers, and part or all of three pay-TV channels.

How They Would Rank
Total 1994 revenues in billions of dollars

Time Warner/ Turner	18.7*
Disney/ABC	16.4
Viacom/ Paramount	10.1
Sony	8.0

*includes Time Warner Entertainment Group

In 1995, Time Warner announced plans to merge with Turner, and Disney announced plans to merge with ABC. This chart shows what their combined incomes would have been in 1994.

- In 1994-95, Oprah Winfrey earned $146 million (US) from her talk show and related activities.

- Advertisers paid $1.2 million for a 30-second TV commercial during the 1995 Super Bowl.

- As of 1994, *E.T.-The Extra-Terrestrial* (1982) had earned more money than any other movie ever made—$399,804,539. In second place, after only one year, *Jurassic Park* (1993) had already earned $356,547,160.

- Rogers Communications Inc., the largest provider of cable TV services in Canada, also owns Maclean Hunter, Rogers Cantel Mobile Communications Inc., YTV, Rogers Pay-Per-View, and Rogers Broadcasting Ltd.

- The Thomson Corporation, based in Canada, owns newspapers and information services in Canada, the U.K., the U.S.A., and 17 other countries around the world. In 1994, it earned more than $5.9 billion dollars (US).

- Torstar Corporation owns Toronto Star Newspapers Ltd., as well as Harlequin Enterprises Ltd., which publishes romance novels in 23 languages and in 1993 sold 200 million books worldwide—roughly six books a second.

- In 1995, The Coca-Cola Company spent more than $134 million on TV advertising in the United States.

- Of the 33.6 million newspapers sold in Canada each week, three companies sell more than half of them: Southam Inc., Thomson Corp., and Toronto Sun Publishing Corp.

Activities

1. To learn about the commercial implications of the media, work as a class and use newspapers, entertainment magazines, and other research sources to find out about the following:
   - the salary of an American and a Canadian network news anchor
   - last year's earnings of the top-five American entertainers
   - the cost of placing a half-page ad in a small community newspaper and a large national newspaper
   - the cost of showing a 30-second commercial on a top-rated prime-time Canadian television show, during the Super Bowl in January, and at 2 a.m. during a movie rerun

2. Using a television guide for one week, look for patterns in prime-time television scheduling between 8:00 and 11 p.m. For example, look at when top-rated programs are scheduled and which shows air at the same time. Suggest possible reasons for the patterns you identify.

3. Research the ownership and influence of Canadian media conglomerates, including Hollinger Inc., Thomson Corp., Southam Newspapers, Rogers Communications, and Bell Canada.

4. Exchange information with classmates about any jobs or other experience you have had with a popular culture or media industry. For example, you might have worked as an usher in a movie theatre, served food in a fast-food chain, or delivered newspapers. Share the knowledge you have gained about the business side of media and popular culture.

Audience

We all have plenty of experience as media audiences. As children we may have watched programs such as *Mr. Dressup* and *Sesame Street*. As we got older we switched to watching news, sitcoms, and dramas, or to reading magazines and listening to the radio. Research indicates that more than seventy-five percent of Canadian homes have cable television, and that each of us spends an average of 190 minutes of our leisure time each day in media or communications activities.

There are two ways of looking at ourselves as media audiences. The first is as consumers of media products, or what is described by the media industry as "target audiences." The second is as active participants, each of us making sense of the media in our own way.

Target Audiences Have you ever become hooked on a television series, only to have it cancelled halfway through the season? The show probably disappeared because it did not bring in its target audience. The media deliver audiences to sponsors, and those sponsors then pay for advertisements within the media texts. The money earned from advertising pays for making the media texts. As target audiences, we are part of a numbers game. For example, a television series needs at least 10 million North American viewers to stay on the air. If the audience numbers drop, the show is cancelled. If the audience grows large enough, the show will be renewed for another season. As a program becomes more popular, the cost of advertising during that show increases, as do the number of people who see the ad. Advertisers are very concerned about the size of their media audiences.

See also
page 74.

See also Video 2,
Excerpt 18.

Hot Spots
Below are the 1994 prices for 30-second prime-time spots, in thousands of dollars (US).

ABC		CBS		NBC		FOX	
Monday Night Football	270	*Due South*	65	*Friends*	140	*Beverly Hills, 90210*	165
Grace Under Fire	215	*Dr. Quinn, Medicine Woman*	150	*Seinfeld*	300	*The X-Files*	80

Active Audiences Have you ever disagreed with a friend about the interpretation of a movie or a TV show? Are you a fan of a performer or rock band that many of your peers dislike? Each of us can get many different and unique meanings from a media text. Our age, gender, social and financial position, family, and life experience can shape our responses to the media. Young fans listening to rap or heavy metal music usually respond quite differently to what they hear than would their parents.

Every time we see or hear a media text, our response is based on the unique elements of our personality and background. For example, many women read Harlequin Romances despite the common belief that these books are sexist and demeaning to women. Researchers have discovered that some women read the books selectively, ignoring stereotypical behaviour and focusing on the moments when women take charge and assert themselves. On a more controversial level, during the highly publicized trial of O. J. Simpson in 1994-95, surveys found that the majority of blacks believed Simpson was innocent while the majority of whites believed he was guilty.

Examples such as these tell us that everyone at times is capable of "oppositional readings" (page 15), resisting the dominant values and messages of the mass media.

Why do we study media audiences? Audience study helps to explain how and why important issues are seen differently by different people, according to their gender, race, and class. If we understand the principles of audience response, we will more easily understand and empathize with other people's ways of thinking. We may also recognize the complexity and contradictions of our own responses to the media.

See also Resource Binder page 79.

Activities

1. Newspapers regularly publish the ratings for the top-ten television programs in the United States and Canada. Compare an American and a Canadian list for the same week and account for any differences you find. What is the audience appeal of the top-rated programs?

2. In your media log, make a list of your favourite TV shows, movies, and music. Then make a list of the ones you dislike. Next, describe a favourite scene from a movie or TV show and

explain why you like it. In small groups, compare your lists and explain the reasons for your choices. Make some general conclusions about how people develop media preferences. Finally, present your group's conclusions to the class in the form of a talk show discussion or a radio phone-in show.

3. Imagine how a family from a completely different background—for example, from a developing nation, or from the Star Trek future, or from 50 years in the past—might interpret some current North American television programs such as sitcoms, soaps, dramas, and tabloid talk shows.

4. Collect or make note of examples of how people use mass media and popular culture products in their daily lives. You might look at how you and your friends use popular culture, or you might examine entertainment magazines and fan clubs and their activities. If you have access to the Internet, find some material from Net sites on popular television programs or rock bands. What do these sources tell you about how audiences use and enjoy popular culture?

For Further Study

1. We can learn a great deal about the history of the twentieth century by examining popular culture. With a group, collect and study a variety of sources of popular culture, such as videos, films, magazines, products, and interviews, that represent different decades from the 1920s onward. Prepare a presentation of your findings for the class. Each group should focus on a different decade.

See also
Resource Binder
page 104.

2. Many independent bands, films, television programs, and alternative magazines exist outside of the large media corporations. Examine some of these media products to find out what value—social, artistic, or commercial—they have to offer. How do the producers or creators pay for and market their products? How might these products change if they were bought out by large media corporations? Share your findings with the class.

See also Video 3,
Excerpt 29.

Chapter Expectations: In this chapter you will learn about

- how media images of men and women can influence your self-image
- how stereotypes used in the media can influence your perceptions of others
- how people make sense of media texts in individual ways
- the issues raised by the portrayal of violence in the media

CHAPTER 2

CONTRAST

Seeing Ourselves: Media and Representation

We live in an image-filled culture. The images the media present to us are on roadside billboards, in hip and trendy merchandise at the mall, and on hundreds of television programs with their endless accompaniment of commercials.

Can you see a trend in the way you and your peers dress and behave? Have the media created an ideal image that you aspire to? How often do you see images of "dumb blondes," "bumbling fathers," and "foreign terrorists" in the media? Examining these media images or "representations" may help you discover what is behind these portrayals. It may also help you to better understand society—and yourself.

representation: *the way groups are presented in the media and popular culture, often through stereotypical images that affect our views of gender, race, class, age, and ability*

"How we are seen determines in part how we are treated; how we treat others is based on how we see them; such seeing comes from representation."
— Richard Dyer, *The Matter of Images*

This chapter explores how we are represented through media images and how that affects the way we see ourselves. It looks at representations of gender, race, youth, and violence.

Key Concepts

Codes and Conventions

The media often use codes and conventions that represent people in stereotypical ways. For example, in family sitcoms on TV, there are stock characters—over-protective mothers, bumbling fathers, and problematic teenagers—who are usually involved in a conflict that, regardless of the severity, must be resolved before the thirty-minute program ends. Program writers and producers feel these stereotyped images convey ideas and actions to the audience better than would more complex representations.

Ideology and Values

How the media tell our stories says a great deal about our values as well as our hidden desires and fears. For example, our concern about law and order is reflected in TV shows that feature lawyers exposing shady deals and injustices. The media also feed on our love for visual images by showcasing the current hot actors and models who personify the "ideal body type."

Industry

To be successful, media professionals must know how to please their audiences. To reach large audiences, they frequently use predictable ways of communicating, such as stereotypes and formulas. But these methods are not foolproof, and producers gauge their success by box office receipts or TV ratings. It is the consumer who ultimately holds the key to the media's power, and who has the influence to change the representations we see.

Audience

Other than for highly publicized events such as the coverage of a world crisis, the Academy Awards, or the Super Bowl, a single media audience does not exist. Instead, there are dozens of smaller audiences, all tuning into different programs, or subscribing to different magazines or newspapers. These smaller audiences, or target audiences, are what advertisers focus on. A target audience might consist of teenage girls, young married couples, or middle-aged men.

On a more personal level, each of us makes sense of media messages in our own unique way. Our interpretation of a film, a TV program, or a rock video will be influenced by our gender, race, class, age, and other factors that are special to each of us.

▲ What codes does this cartoonist use to poke fun at the conventions of high fashion? To what extent does high fashion make women look silly or ridiculous? Give examples to illustrate your answer.

Teen Representation

Teen *Misrepresentation*

probe

What does this still from the movie *Kids* suggest about teens?

As with many groups in society, youth often experience misrepresentation in the media. When the media perpetuate images that are not based on fact, it creates a "media myth." Media myths are usually based on the actions of a small number of people who exhibit extreme behaviour. Here are some examples of media myths.

"Teen pregnancy has reached epidemic proportions."
　　　　　　　　　　—*Time*, May 7, 1990

"Murders and rapes committed by juveniles are on the rise."
　　　　　　　　　　—*Time*, May 7, 1990

"Skyrocketing Teenage Drug Abuse."
　　　　　　　　　　—*Extra*, March, 1994

"Today's young...know less and care less about news and public affairs than any other generation."
　　　　　　　—*Rolling Stone*, November 25, 1993

The headlines and comments above are examples you will likely find in the media today. To what extent do any of them accurately portray you, your school, or your community? How do media images of teens affect your relationships with parents, teachers, police officers, employers, or shopkeepers?

See also page 15.

Representations of Youth: The Look, the Attitude, and the Reality

NBA superstars, cover girls, and rap icons have come to represent youth by promoting a look and attitude that many young people aspire to and identify with. However, on closer examination, these youth heroes pose a real dilemma—are they accurate portrayals or media inventions? Do athletes, models, and musicians in the business of endorsing products represent, distort, or dictate public perceptions of youth?

icon: a highly valued person or product in popular culture like Shaquille O'Neal, Madonna, Coca-Cola, or MuchMusic

While reading the following two selections, decide what came first—the representation or the reality. Do young people pattern themselves after media images or do media images find their inspiration in people like you?

Bad Behaviour Can Prove Profitable

BY JAMES CHRISTIE

If the real source of "attitude" affecting basketball isn't the action, as the National Basketball Association spokesmen claim, what is it?

Most sources in the game pinpoint the marketing schemes of equipment manufacturers, which are as competitive and aggressive as any game on hardwood.

They can take the speed and power of the court and distill it and concentrate it into a message that misbehaviour or intimidation are true badges of manhood —and the route to victory.

During the Christmas season in 1995, the shoe manufacturer Nike ran a commercial of Santa Claus checking a lengthy list of naughty deeds by Dennis Rodman. "But I led the league in rebounds," Rodman counters. "Okay," Santa relents. "Give him the shoes."

Commercials like that can create the impression that bad behaviour can be rewarded—or at least go unpunished— warns former Canadian national team coach Ken Shields.

"There's no value being placed on being sportsmanlike or being a team player," Shields says.

In a recent edition of *Sports Illustrated* that dealt with the issue of misbehaviour

IT'S ABOUT TEAM

GENUINE STARTER STUFF, SEEN ON THE COURT AT WEST 4TH ST.,NYC.

STARTER

▲ Ads like this may affect teen behaviour even more than teen fashion.

in the NBA, the equipment manufacturer Starter placed an ad that ostensibly referred to "team," but definitely conveyed an image of "gang."

It shows a group of young men, mainly minorities, in their loose-fitting gear, standing beside a New York inner-city basketball court. The atmosphere is unfriendly, even intimidating. One white youth is glowering through a chain-link fence and the camera angle is such that the four other muscular young men in the foreground are looking down at the reader—or perhaps a young reader is supposed to be looking up to them. It seems to run counter to the warm, fuzzy psychological ploys that marketers have

traditionally employed to welcome potential customers to the wares.

The ad has an impact, it makes one pause, but the effect may reach beyond sales.

"All I can guess is that the ghetto-type ad is there to appeal to young, white middle-class kids," says Brian Harrod, creative director of the Toronto advertising agency Harrod & Mirlin, analyzing the approaches to basketball-related advertising. His company has no vested interest in basketball clients.

"The black kids in the ghetto can't afford magazines and the literacy rate is not high. It's for the white kid in New Jersey.

"The white middle-class kid may want to be as black as he can in his attitude. He finds excitement there."

But there may be a backlash against the latent hostility of the two types of ads described.

In January 1995, New York agency FBC/Leber Katz Partners created a newspaper ad for Fila equipment, based upon the selection of Detroit Piston rookie Grant Hill as an all-star. The ad cites that when Hill was 12 years old he ran away from his birthday party because he hated being fussed over. He requested his father pick him up in the Volkswagen, because he felt the family's sports car was too showy. And he made the sponsor promise not to make a big deal of the all-star vote. The half-page ad, featuring a soft-focus photograph of Hill's boyish face, appeared once, in *USA Today*. It conveys an unthreatening image of a black basketball player, meant not only to appeal to youths but also their parents, not unlike the personable Michael Jordan.

"The reason for this style goes back to Grant Hill's attitude. He's different from what's out there," says Vonda LePage, a spokesperson for the agency.

"He's grace. He's a nice person. Instead of 'slam, off the rim,' we thought, why not use what he is?

"It comes down to getting a new role model. The message says 'This attitude is A-okay.'"

Doubtless pro basketball would welcome the restoration of that kind of public image. In a few short years, retirements robbed the NBA of several key players who were cornerstones of its growth—Kareem Abdul Jabbar, Larry Bird, and Earvin (Magic) Johnson.

Fila's tactic of using a face and a new style can be as effective as the stop-in-your-tracks glares.

"It's an unwritten rule in advertising that if everyone else is getting into the edginess of ghetto style, you should do something else. You can't fish where everyone else is fishing," Harrod says.

"[The Fila ad] is a good way to zig when everyone else is zagging.

"Violence in sport has been cropping up. Look at Europe, at the suspension of soccer in France, or the karate kick from a player against a fan. Maybe there's a need to get people angry about it."

—*The Globe and Mail*, February 3, 1995

Activities

1. The article describes two ads showing opposite representations of youth. One is rebellious or threatening, while the other shows a clean-cut "good guy." Explain the advertiser's reasons for representing youth in these ways. Which representation do you or your friends aspire to? Which is popular in your school? Why?

2. Clip out an ad from a magazine or newspaper or write a short description of a TV or radio ad for a product associated with athletics. In your media log, explain

- how youth is represented in each ad
- why, in your opinion, the advertiser chose to use this representation of youth
- who the target market is
- why the particular celebrity or model was chosen
- to what extent the ad might influence a teenager to alter his or her image

probe

Some people feel that professional sport has become merely another branch of the entertainment business. With agent-toting athletes negotiating million dollar contracts, franchise owners seeking out the most profitable location for their team, and athletes marketed to youth as media heroes, some have given up on the NBA, NFL, NHL and Major League Baseball. Still others pay big money for tickets and merchandise to support their favourite team.

"We're cheering for laundry," said comedian Jerry Seinfeld, noting that since players constantly change teams, fan loyalty is really to the uniforms.

In your opinion, is professional sport a world of competitive marketing, especially to youth, or is it still a competition based on skill, strategy, and the desire to win?

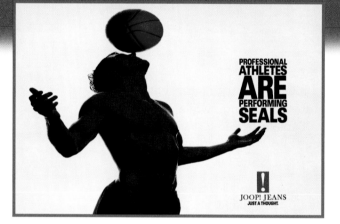

See also Video 3, Excerpt 25.

See also page 97.

Rap Expresses Young People's Anxiety and Joy

BY ROGER McTAIR

What has made rap controversial is the sub-genre of hard-core or inner-city rap. Hard-core rap has emphasized unabashed sexual behaviour toward women, drug use, handgun culture and anti-establishment attitudes.

Like rhythm and blues, like jazz, rap began as a black urban form. In the beginning it was dissed (disrespected) and dismissed by (okay, I'll admit) people my age, and by record companies who didn't know the form would create phenomenal profits. Today, rap is internationally popular. It is obvious something in the form speaks to millions of young people and transcends all kinds of differences.

Rap is a direct descendant of black traditions, some oral, some musical. To rap is to talk well, to preach, both in a secular and religious sense.

On every occasion when black culture has leaped the boundaries of the black community into the mainstream there has been nervousness and denigration. Even in its negative and self-internalized stereotypical forms, the social dynamic behind rap is real. It is a genuine expression of young (black, but obviously not solely black) people's pain, anxiety, contradictions and history.

And, as Marva Jackson, a young rap analyst says, "...their joy. Black youth have few places where they are happy and acceptable. Rap gives them a place to be. And to be joyful. It's their music

and their expression. Some rap is sexist. But society is sexist. Pop music is sexist. And there is very sexist rock music. There is rarely any criticism of pop or rock on those terms. Why only rap?"

Devon, in "Mr. Metro," critiques a difficult relationship with the Metro Toronto Police. And kids are listening to this stuff in North York and Scarborough and Mississauga [suburbs of Toronto]. Then there are the hybrids bhangra, Asian rap and Cockney rap.

Rap is not all obscenity and sexism. But much of what it says is not comforting. It points loudly and impolitely to realities society prefers not to

See also Resource Binder page 66.

hear. The powers that be may not like it, but they should listen to young people's voices, their concerns.

—*The Toronto Star*, January 4, 1994

Activities

1. a) Why might people be critical of rap music?
b) What important roles does rap play for urban youth?

2. a) Bring in the covers of several CDs and/or tapes. Using A Guide to Deconstructing a Visual on page 105 of the Resource Binder, decide what type of image each performer or group is trying to create. How do these representations compare to the lives of the teens who buy the CDs?
b) Design your own CD cover for a real or fictional performer that accurately represents your opinions and values.

3. For an alternate view on why rap has gotten a bad name, read "The Last Days of Rap" on page 34 of the Resource Binder. Consider how rap might be designed to perpetuate racism and negative stereotypes.

Music to Live By

BY JOHN DALY

Music is seen by some as the tie that binds youth culture—in attitudes, values, interests, and tastes. With the emergence of rock and roll in the 1950s, a teen subculture was created, but is it still true, as one writer has said, that "From coast to coast, even from continent to continent, and from disparate ethnic, racial, and religious backgrounds, tens of millions of teenagers share the same visual and aural medium"?

In this 1993 Maclean's *story, John Daly suggests the opposite. He explores how music influences the way we dress, who our peers are, and sometimes how we act. Although the examples in this selection may be dated, the theory of fragmentation is one that is ongoing and useful in studying representation of youth through music.*

Alan Fillingham and the three other members of his rock band, Visions of Insanity, adamantly reject inclusion in any musical category. The Winnipeg high-school students perform songs peppered with high-pitched electric guitar feedback, while others are acoustic- and jazz-influenced. Some of the lyrics explore dark themes like homelessness and alcoholism. When asked to name performers who they admire, drummer Fillingham, singer-guitarist Kyle Gudmundson, lead guitarist Tony Seepish, all 17, and bassist Peter Chodkiewicz, 18, have a diverse list of names ranging from Chicago blues pioneer Muddy Waters to Minneapolis punk rockers Hüsker Dü. Ian Fillingham, a 44-year-old junior-high-school teacher—and a country music fan—says that he is more bemused than offended by his son's taste in music. "I think a lot of it is just an attitude," he says. In fact, across Canada, young people, like their parents, say that music is one of the most important influences in their lives.

Music helps to define dress, hairstyles, companions and gathering places. But unlike their mothers and fathers, teenagers now are splintered into a far greater variety of music-based subgroups. The social groups centred around those diverse and rapidly shifting musical styles vary from city to city, even high school to high school. Music industry executives call the phenomenon fragmentation. Said Paul Alofs, of the HMV Canada record store chain: "In the 1960s and 1970s, you were either into rock 'n' roll or you weren't. Now there is an eclectic range of tastes."

In fact, the term rock 'n' roll is now almost meaningless when applied to music that is popular with teenagers. Alofs has identified 14 distinct styles in the dance/rap category alone, and he split heavy metal into 22 varieties.

That fragmentation is evident at Kelvin High School in south-central Winnipeg, which rock idol Neil Young attended sporadically in the mid-1960s before dropping out. Rebecca Taves, 16, says that there are three principal subgroups at Kelvin: Bangers, Skaters and Alternatives. The Bangers are heavy-metal fans who favour long hair, leather jackets and jeans, while the Skaters are avid skateboarders who dress much like rap fans.

Taves, who looks like a latter-day hippie with her ankle-length red skirt and long straight hair, classifies herself as an Alternative. Many of her favourite artists are folk-influenced. But she adds that the term alternative is a catchall for teens who do not fit into other categories. Taves says that her school also has a small community of preppies, who look as squeaky clean as the term implies, and have more conventional tastes in music.

Whatever musical faction they identify with, most teenagers still share some common tastes. One is a widespread disdain for radio, which in most major Canadian cities is dominated by stations that target 18- to 44-year-old listeners. HMV's Alofs says that both radio stations and record companies are ignoring a huge teen market. He says that teens make up about 60 percent of HMV's customers and in 1992, cassettes by Toronto's Barenaked Ladies and another quirky Toronto group, Moxy Frütvous, as well as the controversial U.S. rap group Public Enemy, all of which received little or no airplay, sold faster in his stores than new releases by such mainstream stars as Madonna, Bruce Springsteen and Michael Jackson.

—*Maclean's*, February 22, 1993

Activities

1. In a small group, describe the "fragmentation" in your own school. How do these groups interact with each other? What are the advantages and disadvantages of having these different groups within your school? How do students in each group choose to represent themselves?

See also
page 174.

2. Daly says that, "Unlike their mothers and fathers, teenagers now are splintered into a far greater variety of music-based subgroups." Record your answers to the following questions in your media log. Include specific examples.
   - Why do you think taste in music has undergone such fragmentation?
   - Are teens less united as a result?

3. Produce a video or radio documentary or write a feature story for your school newspaper on the role music plays in the lives of teens. You may wish to research this topic by surveying a wide variety of students. Ask questions such as
   - What emotions and mood changes do you experience when listening to music?

See also
Resource Binder
page 98.

See also Video 4,
Excerpt 33.

- How does music affect your opinions and attitudes?
- What are the different functions of music, or what different ways do you use music (for example, to relieve boredom or set a mood)?

4. Allan Bloom writes in *Common Culture, Reading and Writing About American Culture* (1995), "Today, a very large proportion of young people between the ages of ten and twenty live for music. It is their passion; nothing else excites them as it does; they cannot take seriously anything alien to music. When they are in school and with their families, they are longing to plug themselves back into their music."

Write a letter to Allan Bloom agreeing or disagreeing with his assessment of the role of music in the lives of young people.

Representations of Race and Stereotypes

See also Video 1,
Excerpts 3, 8,
& 12.

Many people in our society use the term "race" as a convenient way to categorize others or to label people and behaviour, often to maintain an image of superiority or control. Race often includes an impression of dress, accent, or dialect and becomes a kind of shorthand for easy recognition. In the electronic age, it is mostly the media that shape our definition of race. The media also identify issues associated with race such as inequity and racism.

Stereotypes are over-simplified images or representations of people or groups of people. They might be based on race, gender, occupation, or age, and they can be used to justify our popular attitudes and beliefs. There are positive and negative stereotypes, although differentiating between the two can be difficult—a stereotype called "positive" by one group may be found limiting and demeaning by another.

Because familiar stereotypes convey a lot of information quickly, they are frequently used by the media. For example, half-hour sitcoms often use stereotyped characters like the unconventional artist, the rebellious teenager, or the irritable parent to build easy recognition.

It may be easy to spot a stereotype, but it is far more important to uncover the reasons behind its creation. Who benefits from the acceptance of the stereotype and who loses? For example, if adult society sees all teenagers as unstable and unreliable, and the media reinforce that perception through news coverage of juvenile offenders and by stereotyped roles in sitcoms and teen films, then adult society and the media benefit because they don't have to take the time and effort to understand or portray the unique and complex qualities of teenagers. Negative stereotypes very quickly can become part of the accepted way of looking at the world.

See also page 15.

Activity

1. a) In a small group, brainstorm a list of stereotypes you are familiar with, then explain how they may have begun. Be sure to include examples of both positive and negative stereotypes. **b)** Create a collage of familiar media stereotypes, or write and videotape a skit in which you act out or parody several stereotypes.

See also Resource Binder page 80.

Portraits of the "Other"

When we think about people who do not share our background, class, or ethnicity, we tend to look at how they are different from us rather than how they are similar. Below are four categories in which society "slots" those that are different. These categories may overlap and are not exclusive of each other.

The Exotic Aboriginal peoples celebrating in native costumes, Ukrainian folk dancers performing for a Canada Day celebration in Ottawa, African tribesman bringing gifts or performing strange but picturesque rituals for the Queen— these are just some images that might be associated with the "exotic other." When people are identified as "exotic," it suggests that their lives are full of romance, glamour, and excitement.

▲ Chief Justa Monk of the Tl'azt'en Nations greets the Queen in Prince George, B.C.

Through their emphasis on special ceremonies and colourful costumes, media products like *National Geographic* have helped build the notion that African, Asian, and South American peoples are the "exotic other," living lives frozen in time and ritual.

Those that might be considered exotic in Canada are participants in the annual Caribana parade (celebrating Caribbean culture) in Toronto, Ontario, and native people who are "in tune" with the voices of nature and native spirituality.

The Dangerous Dominant groups have long used popular perceptions and exaggerations of the dangerous elements in the "other" to maintain control. The perceived "danger" usually has little support in rational analysis or documented fact—it is mostly the inflated fears, suspicions, and insecurities in the minds of people faced with customs or appearances not familiar to them.

Michael Conrad.

Male. Age 28.

Trafficking.

Armed Robbery.

Assault and Battery.

Extortion.

Rape.

Murder.

Apprehended

January 1994 by

Police Lieutenant

Joseph Cruthers,

shown here.

Urban Alliance
on Race Relations

▶ This ad challenges the image of the "dangerous other."

For example, in North America, some see the "dangerous other" as immigrants—some fear they will take too many jobs or exploit the welfare system.

The Humorous When the "other" are portrayed as humorous, they are often confined to that role—an audience is not apt to take the characters or their concerns seriously. Those that are seen primarily as silly or light-hearted are not usually associated with serious aspirations.

Comedy can also mask racism. Several characters from 1960s and 1970s TV sitcoms are good examples of the "humorous other" reinforcing sexual and racial stereotypes. It's hard to believe now but it was easy to overlook their negative messages. For example, Archie Bunker, in *All in the Family*, was a lovable bigot whose views about blacks, civil rights, and homosexuals were made amusing through his comic performance. Fortunately, other characters, notably Archie's son-in-law, held the opposite beliefs. If possible, watch a rerun of an episode of *All in the Family*, then discuss Archie's character with your classmates.

▲ *Sanford and Son* was the most popular sitcom on NBC from 1972 to 1976.

The Pitied In the 1980s and 90s, the news has been full of horrifying images of famine and mass slaughter, especially from African countries such as Ethiopia and Rwanda. Who can forget

◀ Compare this image of a Somali woman with that found on page 160.

See also page 159.

the sight of thousands of people gathered together, many in the throes of death; of mothers holding their emaciated babies with swollen bellies; and the look of pathos and yearning as the camera pans across the dying multitudes? These pleas for famine relief funds reinforce the notion of Third World peoples as pitiful victims who desperately need our help. The news coverage rarely gives the background of these situations, nor do we see images of the successful farms and thriving businesses which also exist in Africa. By exploiting those in need, the media take power away from them and give it to the media audience.

—adapted from *Learning the Media: An Introduction to Media Teaching*, 1987

See also page 15.

Activities

1. Find examples in several media of all four categories of the "other." In each case, evaluate the impact that each of the patterns of the "other" would have on
   - the person(s) being represented
   - those who create the representation
   - those who view the representation

   Present your conclusions along with a collage or edited videotape of images of the four categories.

2. Choose a magazine and calculate the percentage of advertising that includes representations of visible minorities. In your opinion, what should the percentage be? Explain.

The Arab Stereotype: A Villain Without a Human Face

BY JACK SHAHEEN

Many people criticize television for presenting stereotyped views of minorities. The following article illustrates how the media have reflected a negative view of Arabs.

Portrayed as either billionaires, bombers, or belly dancers, Bedouin bandits or bundles in black—Arabs are hardly ever seen as ordinary people practicing law, driving taxis or healing the sick.

Featured since the early 1900s in more than 500 feature films and scores of television programs, Arabs still lack a human face. The typical screen Arab can be summarized in a handful of clichés: He uses terrorism and/or oil as a weapon against civilized societies. He supposedly worships a different deity than Jews and Christians, and is opposed to both religions. He treats women of his own race as chattel, but prefers to kidnap and rape white, Western women. He delights in the torture of innocents. Although often presented as a coward, at the same time he willingly dies for his cause, because, we are led to believe, he does not appreciate human life as much as "we" do.

Children with Arab roots grow up without ever having seen a human Arab on screen, someone to pattern their lives after. (When 293 secondary school teachers were asked to name any heroic or humane Arab characters they had seen in movies, 287 could think of none.) Instead, they will see animated heroes Heckle and Jeckle pull the rug from under "Ali Boo-Boo, the Desert Rat," and Laverne and Shirley stop "Sheik Ha-Mean-ie" from conquering the U.S. and the world." More than 250 comic books like *The Fantastic Four* and *G.I. Combat* have sketched Arab characters as "low-lifes" and "human hyenas."

Nicholas Kadi, an actor with Iraqi roots, makes his living playing terrorists —the kind of Arab villains who say "America," then spit—in such films as the 1990 release *Navy Seals*, or *True Lies* with Arnold Schwarzenegger. Kadi admits that he does "little talking and a lot of threatening—threatening looks, threatening gestures." The actor explains: "There are other kinds of Arabs in the world. I'd like to think that someday there will be an Arab role out there for me that would be an honest portrayal."

The ugly caricatures have had an enduring impact on Arab Americans. To many during the Gulf War in 1991, all Arabs became "camel jockeys," "rag-heads," and "sandsuckers." Whenever there is a problem in the Middle East, Arab Americans are subjected to vicious stereotyping and incidents of violence and discrimination. Even White House staffers—according to Reagan's first education secretary, Terrel Bell—dismissed Arabs as "sand niggers."

But trends are not uniformly bleak. On television, at least, the worst stereotyping has declined in frequency since the publication in 1984 of my book, *The TV Arab*, when television networks annually aired between 12-22 programs that stereotypically denigrated Arabs. A few recent shows—like *Counterstrike*, *Shannon's Deal* and *Father Dowling Mysteries*—have actually featured sympathetic Arabs and Arab Americans. Perhaps one day it will be possible to retire the stereotypical Arab to a media Valhalla.

—*Extra!*, July/August, 1992

Activities

1. a) Observe how different cultural groups are portrayed on TV over a three-day period and record your findings in your media log. Include programs and commercials in your study.

b) Select one TV program where visible minority characters are in major roles, then evaluate each character from a low of 1 to a high of 7 using the following terms:
- powerful
- likable
- successful
- bad
- good

c) Summarize your conclusions, noting if any of the stereotypes you saw share the same characteristics. If so, explain why. Present your conclusions to the class.

2. In groups, make suggestions that television producers and filmmakers might use to overcome the problem of stereotyping in their programs. Make your suggestions practical and concrete so that they would make a clear difference.

3. An example of the media's ability to stereotype the "other" can be found in their coverage of the 1991 Gulf War. Look for articles, photographs, and cartoons that appeared during this war that might suggest stereotypes. Be sure to note why you consider each item to be an example of stereotyping.

See also page 162.

Linking Media Representations: Gender and Race

Before you begin to explore how the media represent men and women, consider the parallels between representations of gender and race. When studying these representations, ask yourself: Who has power? Who is dominant and who is subordinate?

Historically, men have held the positions of power and earned higher wages. Fortunately, changes have begun to take place in recent years, and women are beginning to experience more equality in the workplace. As well, women are taking the reins of power as university presidents, corporate leaders and prime ministers. However, many women are still lobbying for improvements in gender equity as we move into the twenty-first century.

The quest for racial equality has made a similar journey. Historically, white people have had more privileges than visible minorities. There have been gains in North America, beginning in the 1960s with the civil rights movement in the United States, but like women, visible minorities continue to lobby for equality.

When reading Media and Gender below and Representations of Race and Stereotypes on page 34, consider the similarities between the status of many visible minorities and women. For example, both groups have limited access to social and political power bases in society. When we look critically at media representation, we can see that for every positive gender and race representation, there are just as many representations where women are marginalized or where visible minorities are severely limited by stereotypical mindsets or thinking.

Media and Gender

We have been exposed to gender representations since childhood—in bedtime stories, Saturday morning cartoons, advertising, and films. While the media representations we are exposed to may appear "normal" or accurate, they are constructions that reflect certain values, styles, and ideologies. In studying the images of men and women in the media, we are really examining the constructions of male and female appearance and behaviour that have been selected and created by the producers of a particular text.

Today's popular representations are carefully crafted by designers, photographers, directors, and editors, who use the latest technology available and the codes and conventions of the media to create and shape the stories and images they present.

In recent years, controversy about the effects of media images on men and women has increased. Incidents of eating disorders and steroid abuse have prompted many to examine the role of the media in perpetuating unrealistic standards of beauty. Many wonder how much the media influence the choices we make about our lifestyles and physical appearance, and to what extent media representations help to shape our perceptions of ourselves and others.

**See also
Resource Binder
page 38.**

Body Obsession

BY MARY NEMETH

Mary Nemeth explores how the representation of men and women in the media affects some Canadians. Her investigative report addresses how the images presented by the media affect the way we see ourselves.

The students at Rosedale Heights Secondary School in Toronto do not need a medical journal to tell them what they already know: the pressure to be thin, especially on teenage girls, is often overwhelming. Sitting in a youth worker's office over lunch hour, five attractive girls aged 16 to 19 blame the ubiquitous images of svelte models and actors, as well as comments from peers and siblings. Friends will not say, "You're fat," says Shanel Knoebelreiter, 17. "But they might say, 'Look at that girl, she's so big.' I look and think, 'What are they saying about me?'"

Two of the girls say they used to starve themselves for three or four days at a time, enduring frequent dizzy spells. "People said it would shrink your stomach," explains Tiffany Ruffolo, 16. She finally quit fasting after she fainted. And all five have participated in seminars about body image or related issues. "I think things are changing," says Amanda Sedgwick-Enright, 18. "I don't care any more what society thinks." And when Ruffolo says that she would lose a few pounds if she weren't lazy, Elisha Yoder is quick to challenge her. "That's conditioning telling us that women are lazy when we have meat on our bones," she insists. Still, Yoder, 19, concedes: "It's hard when you intellectually know something and your heart

wants to conform to society's images. It's a conflict within yourself."

Society's ideal image, of course, varies from culture to culture, from generation to generation. Women were expected to emulate the wasp-waisted, corseted look in centuries past, then the dangerous curves of Marilyn Monroe and Jayne Mansfield and later the boyish figure of 1960s model Twiggy. The current crop ranges from waifs to the ample model Anna Nicole Smith. But the ideal, says Dr. Blake Woodside, director of inpatient eating disorders at the Toronto Hospital, are women who have a "totally flat figure except for large breasts, which is physiologically impossible."

Men don't have it easy, either. Men's magazines feature a growing number of articles on body toning and the benefits of healthy living. And the bare male torso has become an advertising staple. The massively muscled Arnold Schwarzenegger-style action hero is a stark contrast to past icons—in the 1930s, even in the movie *Tarzan*, Johnny Weissmuller had a relatively smooth build.

Richard Gruneau, a professor of communications at Simon Fraser University in Burnaby, B.C., notes that, at the turn of the century, images of energetic, athletic young men co-existed with images of portly older men. "Girth was a sign of affluence in the time of the robber barons," he says. As late as the 1960s, adult men did not seem overly concerned with having an athletic body. "The idea of my father being involved in competitive sports as an adult is mind-boggling," says Gruneau, 46. "It would no more have occurred to him than flying to the moon. And he wasn't concerned about the look of his body in the way people are now. He would pat himself and say, 'Gee, I'm packing on a few too many pounds here.' But it was done very informally, haphazardly."

Bodybuilders used to be considered narcissistic, adds Gruneau. It was not until muscle building for strength, rather than appearance, began catching on with football players and other athletes in the late 1960s that it gained respectability. At the same time, professional sports were winning ever wider television audiences, and the athletes themselves were earning ever greater salaries and social status. And then along came Schwarzenegger—the Mr. Olympia featured in the surprise 1976 hit movie *Pumping Iron*—who, Gruneau says, "took that body imagery to the centre of popular culture." There is still a wide variety among celebrated adult male body images, he says. "For every Hulk Hogan," notes Gruneau, "there is a Jean-Luc Picard"—the lean starship captain in *Star Trek: The Next Generation.* But, Gruneau adds, "What's new is that the gym-built body has gained a legitimacy it never had before."

Of course, even back when portly was fine among men, overweight boys suffered schoolyard taunts. "Big people are treated differently," says Stewart O'Neill, 29, who grew up in Halifax and now lives with his wife and son on Lennox Island, off Prince Edward Island. "When I was a kid," says O'Neill, "you'd get called all kinds of names—people can be cruel. It was hard and sometimes it hurt." O'Neill says that he had enough self-confidence to shrug much of it off. But he has encountered negative notions about weight well past childhood. "When you're a big guy, people just want to give you labor jobs, they don't think you can do anything else. It is hard to feel too good about yourself. Let's face it—you don't see too many big people selling stuff on television."

Stephen, a 33-year-old Toronto actor, knows about that. He was 202 pounds when he joined Weight Watchers two months ago, has shed 18 pounds and is hoping to lose another 20. "There is no reason I couldn't do beer commercials or car commercials," says Stephen, who asked that his last name not be used. "But it's very rare you see anyone who's heavier. I guess that's where a lot of the pressure on men comes from—I see it in all the jobs I don't get."

Ultimately, no one can completely ignore the unattainable shapes of a Schiffer or a Stallone, nor stop the next generation of image icons from mounting their pedestals. But it is worth noting that, generally speaking, people are their own harshest judges—and the only ones who can grant themselves a reprieve.

—*Maclean's*, May 2, 1994

1. Review the comments about media images and their effect on self-esteem made in this article. Based on your experience, explain in your media log whether or not you think these comments reflect reality for many teenagers today.

2. In groups, select a particular time period in history (the 1920s or the 1960s, for example) and research the ways in which men and women are represented in the media of the day. Consider the following question in your research:
   - How do you think people from your chosen time period would respond to today's representations of men and women?
   Discuss your findings with the rest of the class. Based on your research, what conclusions can you reach about the representations of men and women over time? Who benefits from the changes in male and female images and fashions?

3. **a)** Examine a variety of current media representations of men and women. For example, view a clip from a movie, a television show or news program, or examine a magazine or newspaper. Analyze the images of men and women presented using the Checklist for Ideology and Values on page 15 as a guide. Based on the examples you examined, what kinds of appearances, behaviours, and attitudes are valued?
   b) Examine one example a second time, analyzing what techniques are used to reinforce content (for example, soft focus, camera angles, and lighting) and what codes and conventions are present.

Gender Roles in the Animated Films of Walt Disney: A Case Study

Walt Disney invented the animated feature film with *Snow White and the Seven Dwarfs*, first released in 1937. For three generations, Disney's animated films have been the primary film experience for children in the industrialized world, and have set the international standard for "family entertainment."

Modern Disney films, just like the classics of the 1930s and 40s, combine realism, fantasy, great mythical themes, interesting characters, and entertaining stories in ways that appeal to children, as well as many older viewers. At the centre of these stories, we see a narrative formula based on the traditional pattern of the hero's quest: the protagonist must confront fear and danger, but in the end, courage and love bring victory.

Many of Disney's heroes and heroines are adapted from fairy tales, and some critics argue that these movies reinforce all the old stereotypes of brave and forceful princes and beautiful but helpless princesses. Others argue that in the most recent Disney films, it is the female characters who have the brains, and the males who end up helpless.

"Our goal is to get a variety of perspectives represented in film and television. Increasing the number of points of view available on screen is not taking anything away from anybody. In fact, it leads to more and better programming, new visions on-screen."

—Joan Pennefather, first woman chair of the National Film Board, in *Maclean's*, March 29, 1993

Activities

1. Select a Disney film and examine the hero or heroine's story closely using the following questions as guidelines:
   - What qualities does the hero or heroine possess? Consider his or her behaviour, attitude, and appearance.
   - Describe the journey he or she must undertake.
   - What lessons does the hero or heroine learn as a result of this journey?
   - What social values are reflected in this film?

2. Create your own proposal for a television program or film that tells the story of a modern hero and answers the questions in Activity 1.

© Disney Enterprises, Inc.

▲ "Someday my prince will come."
—*Snow White and the Seven Dwarfs*

Gender Representation in Advertising

See also Resource Binder pages 36 & 37.

Some people suggest that while the goal of advertising is to convince you to buy a product or accept a message, it also plays a role in shaping attitudes and perceptions about ourselves and the world around us.

The following six codes and conventions are often used in the portrayal of men and women in advertising.

Superiority and Domination In advertising and other media, women are sometimes portrayed in poses that physically subordinate them to men. Men are often shown in a dominant position and in control of the situation being portrayed.

Dismemberment Rather than using full body shots, advertising often chooses to dismember women's and men's bodies and market their separate parts: slim legs, large chest, firm buttocks. This process is often referred to as objectification.

Clowning and Exaggeration In some cases, women are depicted in contorted positions, looking foolish or silly. Men are often portrayed as serious, brooding, and introspective.

Male Approval In some advertisements, women are seen receiving male approval as their sole measure of achievement. Many males depicted in the media approve only one thing—sexually attractive and available women.

The Voice-Over of Authority Men's voices, lower in pitch than women's, are often used in television commercials. A male voice adds authority to the message being delivered. Women are gaining access to positions of authority and the use of female voice-overs is reflective of this change.

Irrelevant Sexualization of Women and Girls Advertisers have often used sex to sell products, even when the product being advertised has nothing to do with sex. Car, alcohol, soft drink, and jeans ads often market women's bodies as well as the actual products being advertised.

—adapted from MediaWatch, *Trends in the Media Portrayal of Women in the Media*

Activity

1. Examine several current TV and print ads.

a) Deconstruct these ads using the six codes and conventions described above and the Checklist of Ideology and Values on page 15.

b) What effect do these codes and conventions have on the messages in the ads?

c) Based on your conclusions in a) and b), decide how accurate these codes and conventions are. Should some be deleted or others added?

Sexual Stereotyping: Women Respond

In June of 1994, MediaWatch, a feminist media watchdog organization, conducted a survey of 625 women to find out how women in general respond to offensive advertising that may portray sexual stereotyping. They received the following results:

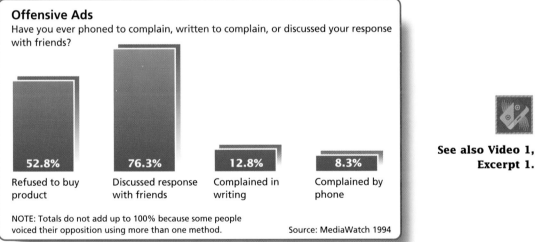

Offensive Ads

Have you ever phoned to complain, written to complain, or discussed your response with friends?

52.8%	76.3%	12.8%	8.3%
Refused to buy product	Discussed response with friends	Complained in writing	Complained by phone

NOTE: Totals do not add up to 100% because some people voiced their opposition using more than one method.

Source: MediaWatch 1994

See also Video 1, Excerpt 1.

"In an increasingly competitive marketplace, sexism may be becoming an unaffordable luxury."

"The study on television advertising is a wake-up call to marketers who turn a blind eye to women's distaste of sexual stereotypes."

—Shari Graydon, former MediaWatch president, in *The Globe and Mail*, October 27, 1994

SEEING OURSELVES: MEDIA AND REPRESENTATION | **47**

See also
Resource Binder
page 116.

1. Using the statistics in the MediaWatch survey, write a short news story outlining some of the findings. Share your story with your classmates.

2. Design a television or magazine ad for jeans, perfume, or cosmetics, using positive representations of women and men. Explain what elements in the ad will achieve this positive representation.

Media Controversy: Sexual Images

See also
Resource Binder
page 42.

Certain elements used in advertising and other media are considered by some to be pornographic. But no agreement has ever been reached to define what pornography is or to define the distinction between the erotic and the pornographic. However, it is important to recognize that certain values that are found in pornography also appear in the mainstream media. Examine the chart below and use it to evaluate several images from the media. Explain why people may be especially concerned with these kinds of images.

Value	Mainstreaming of Value
Innocence may be the last frontier (the sexy virgin).	The "pretty baby syndrome," or the youth focus of advertisements. Look for advertisements of children's clothing to see if they are sexualized.
Pain may be pleasurable.	The scene in *Gone With the Wind* with Rhett Butler and Scarlett O'Hara on the staircase. Look for advertisements that imply violence.
If women could choose, they would sell sex whenever they could.	This is the meaning behind many advertising pitches (for example, buy the car and the smiling woman comes with it).
When men dominate, the result is both natural and sexy, and women enjoy being dominated in this way.	The macho male character in many heavy metal videos and action films.
Women are sexual objects to be looked at and played with.	The image of women in men's magazines, on soap operas, and on fashion television.

—adapted from Ontario Ministry of Education, *Media Literacy, Intermediate and Senior Divisions*, 1989

1. **a)** Examine examples of male and female images from the media that you consider controversial. What makes these images controversial? Use the Checklist of Ideology and Values on page 15 and the chart on page 48 to examine the use of sexual images in your examples. Consider the influence of these values on the message of the ad and on the audience.
b) Discuss the possible reasons for the popularity of images some people consider offensive.

2. Find examples from the media that present alternatives to controversial images of sexuality. Discuss what makes these images different.

3. As a consumer, you can voice your opinion on the kinds of representations you would like to see. Choose one of the examples from the media you have studied and write a letter that expresses your approval or disapproval of the gender image portrayed. Consult page 81 of the Resource Binder for tips on letter writing.

Ridiculing the Ridiculous: Adbusters' Spoofs

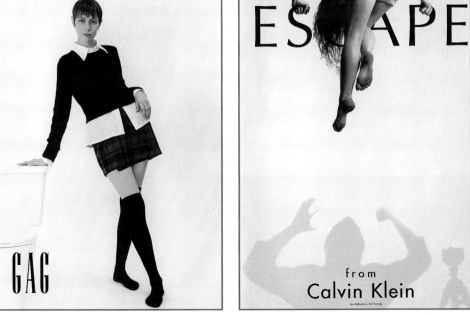

▲ What messages do these *Adbusters*' spoof ads convey about our consumer society?

Adbusters magazine, published by the Media Foundation in Vancouver, B.C., contains several examples of ads that spoof mainstream advertising campaigns, including the Gap and Calvin Klein spoofs on the previous page.

See also Video 3, Excerpt 29.

- Examine these examples and evaluate the effectiveness of using humour to make a critical point.

- Try creating your own television commercials or print ads that imitate the intent and style of an *Adbusters'* spoof.

The Retouching Epidemic

BY
MARSHALL BLONSKY

In examining the representation of men and women in advertising and fashion magazines, it becomes obvious fairly quickly that the images are dominated by a particular type of man and woman. Generally speaking, most ads feature young, attractive, white, or "white-looking" men and women. These men and women are fit and slim, have clear complexions and near-perfect features.

But do models really look like this? Just how is this picture-perfect world achieved? New technology has changed the ways in which media images can be created, but these changes have not occurred without controversy.

It was December 10, 1990—no war yet in the Persian Gulf, but the tension was thick—and *Time* magazine's cover was an American Marine bathed in a radioactive red haze. The shot, *Time* admitted on the contents page, was computer retouched to heighten the cover's drama: "What War Would Be Like."

Well, now we know what the war was like, more or less. But what no one knows is where the dazzlingly manipulative photo-retouching technology used by *Time*—as well as by just about every other magazine and many newspapers—will take us. How drastically will it change the images we see, pictures of everything from cosmetics to Kuwait?

Computers have made retouching and the complete re-creation of photos so fast and efficient that photo technicians have now joined video and recording engineers in the fraternity of modern manipulators, each of them capable of reassembling bits of reality for any effect at all.

In women's magazines, models can be electronically massaged into visions more idealized than ever before. Dot by microscopic dot, the computer operator can create a new photograph, leaving no trace of his handiwork. The computer-retouching systems—Scitex, Quantel Graphic Paintbox, Du Pont Crosfield—make it temptingly easy to remove every wrinkle from an aging celebrity, turn yellow skin pink, substitute one model's hair for that of another. They can widen eyes, reduce breasts, put a different swimsuit on someone, even move the sun if it's in the way.

The power and ease of the new technology has led to edgy criticism of the media by many of its own members. The critics are often photographers who have recoiled in the face of retouching. Today, they say, retouchers are going so far, they are obliterating reality with a technology that begs to be abused. The potential for abuse has prompted not only alarm but also soul-searching among editors and others in the media.

How much is too much? Although retouching of photographs has been common for decades, at what point is the faith in photography's ability to convey reality hurt beyond healing? It's an ethical issue that becomes all the more muddled when we cross from fantasy photos of movie stars and models to Marines in the field. Are celebrity photos as sacrosanct as news photos?

"Some editors used to be loath to retouch too much," says Fred Ritchin, a former *New York Times Magazine* photo editor who is sounding the alarm. "But now that it's so easy, some editors do it in more massive ways. They don't want to settle for reality the way it looks. They want it the way they want it—and the way they think the reader would like it. They have a huge amount of power."

But when I spoke to photographer Eric Boman about some of the grosser distortions, particularly on magazine covers, he scoffed. "Don't be naive— cover photographs have never been photographs. I used to do covers for

years, and they're nothing but expressions made into graphic design. You make the girl look as come-hither, as glowing, happy, healthy, and beautiful as possible. You barely see it is Shirley MacLaine on the cover. You see the color they've poured into the expression—the red, the shocking pink, or the orange."

Still, there is a significant difference now. With the former method, hand retouching, technicians sprayed or brushed the paint or dye over the surface of the print or transparency. A lot could be done and a lot always was, but now hand retouching seems quaint compared with the possibilities of the computerized version. The Paintbox system or its equivalent provides up to 16 million colors. In the digitized world of the computer, a photograph becomes raw material for a technician who can take its elements and exaggerate them, diminish them, enhance them, or eliminate them. And photographer and computer retoucher Barry Blackman couldn't be happier. Now, he says, "I have the same freedom to work with photographic images that illustrators have had for centuries. I am no longer hindered by the laws of physics and the laws of reality." Not hindered by the laws of reality? It's this kind of insouciance that drives the people alarmed by computerized retouching into paroxysms of fury.

In the last three years, as technology has been refined and prices have declined, hundreds of companies have bought the computer systems, including more than 25 newspapers and an untallied number of magazines. Reportedly, the number will grow to 1,500 companies in the next five years. From the point of view of magazine and

On the labeled photo:
- BRIGHTEN BLUE OF EYES
- REMOVE HOLE IN EAR
- KEEP BRIGHT COLOUR OF HAIR
- ERASE BLEMISHES AND FRECKLES
- SMOOTH WRINKLES ON NECK
- SMOOTH DIMPLE ON NOSE TIP

On the magazine cover:
allure
APRIL 1991 $2.50
L.A. BEAUTY
All-Natural Artifice
Secret Lives of THIN French Women
HAIR OF THE MOMENT
GET METAPHYSICAL SPAS
MAKEUP
Meet Your Match

▶ On this *Allure* cover, the model's arm was lengthened and her eyelashes were drawn on.

newspaper art departments, the machines are irresistible.

"Conventional color retouching has always been expensive and time-consuming," says Ritchin. "The computer's advantage is that it operates instantaneously. You see your results immediately. You don't give an image to somebody and wait three days for it to come back." But Ritchin, who has exposed some of the technology's abuses in his book, *In Our Own Image*, is troubled by what he believes is an assault on documentary photography.

It was the late critic Roland Barthes who wrote that the photograph is like the gesture of a child "pointing his finger at something and saying: *that, there it is*." Now, with the new power to manipulate what happens after the camera points and shoots, we have, in Ritchin's view lost our reality check—if the photograph is thought of as a plaything to be retouched, then when real photographs tell us something serious in the future, who's going to believe them?"

He's talking about photojournalism in this instance, about the photographs that came out of Tiananmen Square, for example, but he fears for all photography. "What people don't understand is that if photojournalism erodes, all other photography erodes—fine artwork, beauty, advertising. If people stop believing the documentary, they'll believe less in other kinds of photography, Madonna covers, advertisements."

Madonna's *Glamour* cover of December 1990 is a widely discussed case in point. Her teeth were bleached, and lines in her face were erased. Her publicist, Liz Rosenberg, recalls that Madonna looked at an early version of the cover and said, "Oh, my God, look what they did to my teeth! It looks like they glued them together, up and down and across." Rosenberg tried to stop publication but failed. It wasn't that Rosenberg is against remaking a person's looks (we're talking about Madonna here), it's just that the star didn't like the result.

"I think entertainment—and *Glamour* is entertainment—is all about looking great," Rosenberg says. "If it makes the artist look great, why not? Any picture of any artist on Warner Brothers that comes in, I can't get to the Quantel Graphic Paintbox fast enough."

Now that the flap has died down, *Glamour* editor-in-chief Ruth Whitney describes it all as a practical decision. "As in any electronic retouching," she says, "they were making an effort to hold the white of Madonna's teeth. I looked at that cover dozens of times [before publication], and I didn't notice anything. It's true that once you focus on the teeth you keep on seeing them. But we never noticed it. I'm just glad it's all over," she says, laughing.

A more drastic alteration of Madonna's looks was accomplished by David Rickerd at Applied Graphics Technologies while he was working on the *Vogue* cover of May 1989. In the photo, Madonna sits on the step of a swimming pool, partly submerged, glancing over her shoulder. "Here's what I've done in the retouching," says Rickerd as he looks at his work again. "I changed the color of her lips—made them brighter red instead of a deep red—whitened her teeth, color-corrected her hair where she had those bleached-out streaks on top of her head. I made the hair more of an even brown. As you see, I narrowed the strap on her swimsuit to bring it into fashion." Most daringly, he removed her legs, still visible beneath the water, along with the side of her breast that could be seen as she swiveled to look backward. Although this cover appeared before the *Glamour* photo, there was, surprisingly, no controversy. Madonna must have liked it.

The implications for such vigorous manipulation of photographs go beyond issues of truth and fantasy to influence how women view themselves. Fabien Baron, a former art director of Italian *Vogue* who is now in advertising in New York, says that the computer has turned a woman's body into something like fashion itself, even if changing it is a bit more difficult. "If a woman wants to be perfect—and the manipulated images tell her she has to be—then she has to be cut in 15 places. She has implants and collagen and fat suction and cut this and cut that."

Baron believes that modern photo retouching has gone over the top. "The images are plastic," he says. "They are hyper-real. What's gone out of fashion photography is portraiture. Formerly, when Penn and Avedon were younger, almost every picture was a portrait. The model didn't have to be perfected; she could have character." He picks up a magazine. "There's no portraits," he says as he flips through the pages. "I know I won't find a single one. I don't even know why I'm looking."

—*Allure*, September, 1991

Activities

See also page 184.

1. a) Describe how retouching techniques are used in print media.
b) What are the advantages of computer retouching?
c) What objections are there to these techniques from people in the industry? Do you agree or disagree with these objections? Explain.

2. a) What impact do you think the kinds of manipulated images mentioned in the article have on women and how they see themselves? Explain your responses.
b) "How much is too much?" Does your knowledge of computer retouching make you feel differently about the images you see in magazines? In your media log, write a few short paragraphs outlining whether or not you feel computer retouching has gone too far. Be sure to offer examples to support your conclusions.

3. a) If you have access to the appropriate equipment in your school, either have someone take your picture using a digital camera, or scan your image from a photo into a computer. Experiment with some of the new photo manipulation software to alter your appearance. What kinds of changes does the software make possible? What effect can these changes have on your image?
b) If you do not have access to this equipment, research to find out about any advances in the technology for altering images. You might consult a local computer store, or approach an advertising firm, or the art department of a publishing house or magazine.

4. Clip out several pictures of your favourite actress or actor from magazines, then compare how the person looks in each photograph. What examples do you see of photo retouching? Are the images touched up differently? Which photograph looks most natural? Why?

Media and Violence

If you think about how people are represented by the media, the issue of violence may not be the first thing that comes to mind. But the portrayal of people involved in violent acts is one of the most controversial issues in the media and it is represented almost everywhere you turn. And for most people, viewing violence is a guilty pleasure.

It is not hard to find violence: it is all around us, in movies, television, sports, music, and video games. Take a few moments to brainstorm examples of violence from these or other media products.

Because violence is so pervasive, many people have begun to lobby against it, calling for its censorship. Many of these people believe that the representations of violence in the media influence the rest of society to become more violent. In response to these concerns, the federal government enacted a violence code for broadcasters in 1994 that lays down several restrictions including the following: "Programming for children shall not contain realistic scenes of violence which create the impression that violence is the preferred way, or the only method, to resolve conflicts between individuals."

Studies have not provided conclusive answers to the question of whether media violence is responsible for real-life violence. Research shows that children are more aggressive with their toys after watching music videos, and less aggressive after watching nature programs, but that is only in a controlled situation. What researchers say is that when children are at home, they may try to act aggressively after watching violence, but that parents, older siblings and baby-sitters limit their "bad" behaviour.

Some people believe that media violence teaches viewers how to commit crimes. Research has not been able to prove this claim either. In fact, real-life violence is often motivated by the impact of poverty, unemployment, anger, and frustration.

What research *can* validate is that heavy television viewers believe that their communities are less safe now than ten years ago, even if the amount of crime has in fact decreased. This belief has been termed "the mean world syndrome," a phenomenon that shows us projecting our frustrations about law, authority, and our perceptions of world decline onto the media. In turn, these projections come back to us in the form of violence on television, in movies, sports, music, and video games.

The Taste Test

BY LOUISE BROWN

Louise Brown wrote this article as though children's programming was on trial for being too violent. In the role of a defence lawyer, she objects to efforts to control children's television.

Your Honor, my client has heard the government's plan to ban all cartoons from Saturday morning television and replace them with marathons of *Hinterland Who's Who*, and she respectfully wishes to object.

Ever since controversy erupted last year over the effect of *Power Rangers* on young viewers, this government has been besieged with requests for program prohibitions. Even *Fred Penner's Place* has come under attack for encouraging children to invade a forest glen and disrupt the natural habitat.

My client, Toronto author Kathleen McDonnell, wishes to state that she sympathizes with parents' wishes that children not grow into violent adults. As a feminist mother of two daughters, McDonnell is concerned with the heavy reliance on violence to spice up children's entertainment, as well as the absence of strong female role models in children's books and TV.

See Video 1, Excerpt 2.

But Your Honor, in her recent book, *Kid Culture: Children and Adults and Popular Culture*, McDonnell argues that parents are overestimating the influence TV can have on kids if there is a balance of other activities in their lives, from fresh air to music, books and imaginative play.

My client submits that children can be trusted not to simply mimic everything they see on TV—if their parents make time to talk with them often about the family's real values such as respect, equality and non-violence.

And while she agrees Saturday morning cartoons are often one long toy commercial for related merchandise, they do have other redeeming features and must not be dismissed as a genre simply because they plug action figures during the breaks. My client would draw your attention to the growing presence of female characters in action cartoons. Although for a long time this genre was almost exclusively male save for the odd female in need of rescue, this pattern began to change in the early 1980s with the arrival of *She-Ra, Princess of Power*, the first female to break the glass ceiling of the superhero world.

In the 1990s there has been a quiet revolution of strong female characters infiltrating such shows as *X-Men, Mighty Morphin Power Rangers, Captain Planet* and *Where In The World Is Carmen Sandiego?* (whose elusive female villain is known as the "world's greatest thief").

Of the eight X-Men, four are women, and they do plenty of rescuing as well as being rescued, as do the female Power Rangers and Planeteers. And although these shows rarely try to be educational in a didactic sort of way, parents who sit through them might be surprised at the social issues addressed, from pollution to racial prejudice.

The X-Men, for example, often are attacked by narrow-minded people who denounce them for being different, and one episode even had the X-Men unfairly blamed for the spread of a new plague—unmistakable echoes of AIDS and the spectre of homophobia.

Some parents will argue these themes are too subtle for kids, but my client would argue that allegory and fable are time-honored genres for conveying morals to children. Too, these shows often have a refreshingly international perspective, with some superhero team members hailing from developing countries, not just the United States.

As for the increasingly smart-aleck humour found in the new generation of cartoons, McDonnell agrees that with *Animaniacs*, producer Steven Spielberg has crossed the line from a modern cartoon anchored in narrative and slap-stick humour, to create an orgy of hip irony more suited to adults than kids.

As many media experts have said, my client puts to the Court that instead of worrying so much about what their children watch, parents should limit how much TV kids watch, to allow time for other activities—even fantasy games based on those TV shows.

But within the permitted ration of TV, parents should let kids control what she calls the "Kid's Culture Menu," as long as it's not something that would frighten the child or introduce him to concepts inappropriate for his age.

McDonnell submits that no matter how unsavory cartoons may seem to well-meaning parents, children should be entitled to their own culture, even if it offends our middle-class, educated sensibilities.

Indeed, Your Honor, a "taste gap" between parent and child is a necessary part of growing up. Just ask any baby boom parent who used to watch *The Monkees* or *Shindig*.

—*Starweek Magazine*, January 7, 1995

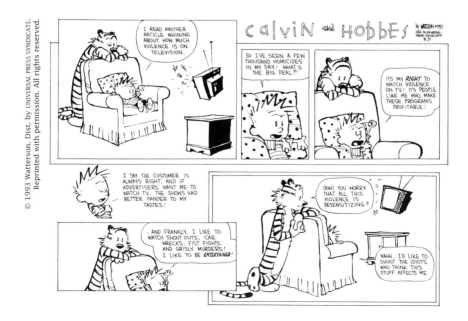

1. Why do you feel the author wrote her essay as a courtroom trial? Does it make her essay more effective or less effective? Be sure to offer reasons to support your opinion.

2. In your media log, explain the author's viewpoint on violence in children's cartoons. Do you agree with her? Why or why not? Compare her opinion to the message in the *Calvin and Hobbes* cartoon.

3. As a class, role-play a court case that charges a television network with influencing children to be violent. You will have to assign the roles of judge, crown attorney, defendant, defence lawyer(s), plaintiff, jury, court stenographer, and so on.

4. After rereading the essay, try to write a piece that takes an opposing viewpoint. You may wish to do research before you begin by talking to parents who believe that television for children is too violent.

TV Isn't Violent Enough

BY MIKE OPPENHEIM

While many television critics say that programs show too much blood and gore, Mike Oppenheim argues that there isn't enough. Not enough, at least, to portray the consequences of violence realistically.

The trail of quiet corpses left by TV's good guys, bad guys and assorted ill-tempered gun owners is ridiculously unreal. A pistol is certainly a deadly weapon, but not predictably so. Unlike a knife wound, one bullet can kill instantly—provided it strikes a small area at the base of the brain. Otherwise, it's no different: a matter of ripping and tearing enough tissue to cause death by bleeding. Professional gangland killers understand the problem. They prefer a shotgun at close range.

No less unreal is what happens when T. J. Hooker, Magnum or a Simon brother meets a bad guy in manly combat. Pow! Our hero's fist crashes into the villain's head. Villain reels backward, tipping over chairs and lamps, finally falling to the floor, unconscious. Handshakes all around . . .

Sheer fantasy! After hitting the villain, our hero would shake no one's hand. He'd be too busy waving his own about wildly, screaming with the pain of a shattered fifth metacarpal (the bone behind the fifth knuckle), an injury so predictable it's called the "boxer's fracture." The human fist is far more delicate than the human skull. In any contest between the two, the fist will lose.

The human skull is far tougher than TV writers give it credit. Clunked with a blunt object, such as the traditional pistol butt, most victims would not fall conveniently unconscious for a few minutes. More likely, they'd suffer a nasty scalp laceration, be stunned for a second or two, then extremely upset. I've sewn up many. A real-life, no-nonsense criminal with a blackjack (a piece of iron weighing several pounds) has a much better success rate. The real-life result is a large number of deaths and permanent damage from brain hemorrhage.

Critics of TV violence claim it teaches children sadism and cruelty. The critics have it backward. Children can't learn to enjoy cruelty from the neat, sanitized mayhem on the average series. There isn't any! What they learn is far more malignant: that guns or fists are efficient, exciting ways to deal with a difficult situation.

Truth in advertising laws eliminated many absurd commercial claims. I often daydream about what would happen if we had "truth in violence"—if every show had to pass scrutiny by doctors who could insist that any action scene have at least a vague resemblance to medical reality. ("Stop the projector! You have you hero waylaid by three thugs who beat him brutally before he struggles free. The next day he shows up with a cute little bandage over his eyebrow. We can't pass that. You'll have to add one swollen eye, three missing teeth, at least 20 stitches over the lips and eyes and a wired jaw. Got that? Roll 'em.")

Seriously, real-life violence is dirty, painful, bloody, disgusting. It causes mutilation and misery, and it doesn't solve problems. If we're genuinely interested in protecting our children, we should stop campaigning to "clean up" TV. It's already too antiseptic. Ironically, the problem with TV violence is that it's not violent enough.

—*TV Guide*, March 31, 1984

Activities

1. What does the author mean when he says that "the problem with TV violence is that it's not violent enough"? In your media log, explain why you agree or disagree with this statement.

2. According to the author, what effect does sanitized violence have on children? Discuss whether you agree with the solution he proposes and why. Suggest other possible solutions.

3. How are fights in TV shows and films staged to mask the reality of their violence? Consider special effects, sound effects, choreography, and music. To what extent does the knowledge of these kinds of special effects lessen the impact of the violence?

Does Violence Make a Good Movie?

Many people are concerned about the amount of violence in today's movies, especially the action and adventure genres that are popular with young audiences. It seems that few movies today—except for those specifically for children—are being made without the customary fight scenes, car chases, shoot-outs, knife fights, and technicolour explosions of people and property. Below are five reasons why we see so much violence, and why we're likely to keep seeing it in the future.

1. Movies, by their very nature, are about movement, and some of the most exciting kinds of movement involve violence.

Most viewers want to exercise their emotions, and violence is one of the easiest ways to produce emotional thrills or jolts. Many people watch violent movies for the same reason that they ride roller coasters—the experience may be terrifying, but it's never boring.

▲ Which of the five reasons for violence could apply to this scene from the movie *Fair Game*, starring William Baldwin and Cindy Crawford?

2. Movies are made with a young audience in mind.

Filmmakers study their audience profiles carefully, and they know that young people account for eighty percent of ticket sales, even though they are only twenty-five percent of the overall population. Unlike adults, young viewers will also watch their favourite films over and over again, often renting the video of a film they enjoyed originally on the big screen. Action and horror films, with high levels of explicit violence, have proven to be popular with young audiences.

3. Production companies want a good return on their multi-million dollar investments.

Recent history shows that violent movies make money, and that very violent movies make the most money. American exports dominate the "big budget" market, not only in Canada, but around the world, and successful international sales are often necessary for these films to make a profit. Since violence is internationally understood, distributors like to stick with what sells.

4. Movies can portray violence with spectacular realism through the use of computerized special effects.

However, as audiences become accustomed to more and better effects in each new movie, producers have to outdo their competitors by developing even more spectacular effects. Thus, big budget films—in which millions have been invested in the special effects alone—can make their small budget competitors seem dull and boring. So when we pay to see a big budget extravaganza with great special effects, we send a clear message to producers that this is what we want, and as a result, this is what we get.

5. Historically, stories have contained a hero and a villain and any conflict between them is resolved by violence.

This "formula" goes back to the hero myths of ancient cultures and reinforces the perpetual rift between good and evil. For example, Hercules and Thor vanquished their opponents through violence, not negotiation.

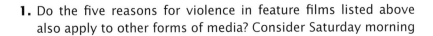
Activities

1. Do the five reasons for violence in feature films listed above also apply to other forms of media? Consider Saturday morning

See also
Resource Binder
page 96.

cartoons, police dramas, and music videos.

2. In deconstructing media violence, we must examine the situation in which violence occurs. In some situations, violence may seem necessary for realism. In others, it may seem unnecessary and intrusive. In groups, decide whether the following scenarios are justified or not in their use of violence. Be sure to offer reasons and examples to support your conclusions. It is not necessary that your group reach a consensus.

- A nature program on television shows footage of lions killing and eating their prey.
- A feature film depicts a stabbing, and the long drawn-out torture of a man who was guilty of several murders.
- A made-for-TV movie drama about wife-battering shows graphic scenes of a man hitting his wife.
- A distraught woman decides to commit suicide by jumping from a building and a TV camera records the event for an evening newscast.
- A newscast shows footage of a prisoner in a war-torn region being jeered at and stoned by a large crowd and dragged around a town square.

Chapter Summary

Because it includes gender, race, and class, the territory of representation is extensive: from Barbie dolls to action films, from racial stereotypes to the special viewpoints of teenagers. We live in a complex world in which many voices are struggling to be heard and respected, whether they are the voices of women, visible minorities, or the elderly. This struggle for equality is essential for fostering a democratic society with fully participating citizens. The media can play a significant role in this struggle by ensuring that its representations are fair and unbiased.

Summary Activities

Codes and Conventions

1. What codes and conventions do the media use most frequently to represent the following:
   - relationships between teenagers and their parents
   - families in developing nations
   - a young man wearing the latest fashion

Ideology and Values

2. Watch a variety of television dramas and sitcoms, paying attention to the endings of the stories. Brainstorm the ideology and values offered in each program.

Industry

3. Many films and television shows targeted to specific groups fail at the box office. Explain why this happens so frequently and what lessons these failures may provide for the media industry.

Audience

4. Choose two popular music bands representing two different musical styles. Write a short description of the characteristics of each band's audience, noting how the bands target their music to each group.

For Further Study

5. In your opinion, are there some similarities between the issues of media and race, and media and gender? In your media log, explain what the similarities and/or differences are, noting examples to support your conclusions. You may wish to reread the descriptions of the "other" on page 35 as well as the material on gender on page 41 before you respond.

6. a) Examine magazine ads that use representations of youth, race, gender, or violence to sell products. Using the Checklist of Ideology and Values on page 15, deconstruct these ads and answer the following questions:
- What are these ads selling?
- Are any implied messages being conveyed to audiences? If so, what are they?
- What kind of impact do you think these ads will have on particular audiences?

b) Evaluate the ad based on the Canadian Advertising Foundation's Gender Portrayal Guidelines on page 42 of the Resource Binder. You may wish to write a letter to the foundation in which you outline the ways in which the advertiser has or has not complied with the guidelines.

7. Select other groups not included in this chapter and indicate the problems and/or advantages associated with their representation. Using the Checklist of Ideology and Values on page 15, indicate who gains power and who loses it because of the ways they are represented. Some examples of these groups might be
- baby boomers
- environmentalists
- skin heads
- Florida tourists
- rural people
- rollerbladers

8. The image of "cool" for youth has varied over the years. In groups, define what would qualify as "cool" today. What are some media representations, current or past? Look at Elvis Presley in the 1950s, or James Dean and Marilyn Monroe, or at current stars like Brad Pitt, John Travolta, Will Smith, Drew Barrymore, and Winona Ryder. Use your definition of "cool" to create an ad for a consumer product or a promotional poster for a teen film.

9. Wearing team logos on clothing is a common code representing a loyal team supporter. However, many people wear logos just to be in style. Prepare and conduct an interview between a school newspaper or radio reporter and a student who wears many logos. Have the student explain the reason for his or her clothing choices. Record or write a report of the interview.

10. As a class, summarize the main insights you have gained about representation. Write five recommendations for people who work in media industries to follow in order to overcome being accused of misrepresentation.

Chapter Expectations: In this chapter you will learn about

- how advertising can manipulate your emotions, ideas, values, and actions
- how advertisers identify and speak to specific target audiences
- how corporate sponsorship may influence your education
- how public relations techniques are used to create positive images for corporations and institutions

CHAPTER 3

Selling Images and Values

Advertising surrounds us. It's everywhere: on radio and television, on billboards and stadium walls, on T-shirts, knapsacks, and designer jeans. But the art of persuasion is not limited to advertising. Our lives are also influenced by lifestyle promotions, corporate sponsorships, marketing, and public relations campaigns. The chart on page 83 illustrates some of the influences you probably face every day at school and in your community.

In this chapter, you will be asked to think about such questions as: When you buy a pair of jeans or shoes, are you buying something you really want, or something you have been persuaded to want? Who benefits when corporations sponsor school teams or buy the exclusive rights to sell their products in your school?

Advertising and public relations campaigns use time-honoured methods of persuasion to promote products and services, to change people's behaviour, and to influence their values and beliefs. The goal of this chapter is to alert you to both the obvious and the subtle persuasive messages that surround you. As media consumers, it is important for you to recognize these messages so that you can understand their influence on your actions, beliefs, and values.

Key Concepts

Codes and Conventions

Happy families gathered around the dining room table; slim, beautiful women posed seductively; attractive and active young adults playing sports or sitting around a campfire—these images are samples of codes used in advertising. Advertisers skillfully use words, pictures, and sound to create images with strong emotional appeal. One of the most famous advertising campaigns is the simple but powerful image of the Marlboro man, a cowboy riding the range who embodies the codes of the American West: freedom and rugged independence.

Ideology and Values

Many people say that the images and ideas in advertising simply reflect those of our society. But critics of advertising point out that ads create artificial needs and manipulate our emotions to encourage us to buy. Many advertisers present their products as tickets to emotional fulfillment and social acceptance. What do you think? Do ads simply provide us with information about the products we buy, or do they promise us power and social success if we buy the right things?

Industry

Advertising is a multi-billion dollar business whose main goal is to sell products, services, and ideas. Manufacturers often spend as much or more to sell a product as to make it. Money paid by advertisers finances most magazines and newspapers and most of the programming on radio and TV. Despite all the money involved in producing an advertising campaign, it is still hard to guarantee success. Advertisers try to avoid failed campaigns by focusing their advertising on very specific targeted groups: for example, families with young children or single professionals with plenty of disposable income.

Audience

See Video 1, Excerpts 8 & 12.

Advertisers study different target audiences through surveys, focus groups, and in-depth interviews, in order to identify existing consumer needs. They then create advertisements that appeal to specific groups of people. However, most North American advertising is aimed at white middle-class people, while minority groups are frequently ignored. It is important to realize that each of us responds differently to advertising messages, depending on our gender, race, class, and personal experiences.

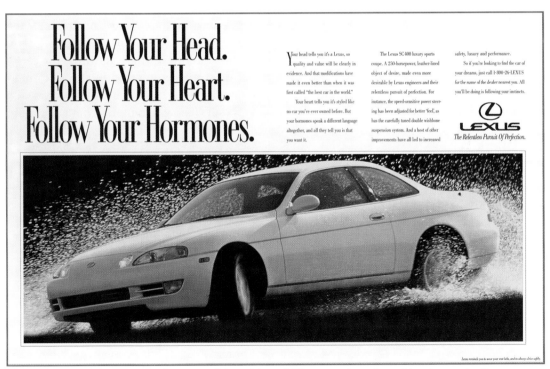

▲ Who do you think Lexus is hoping will buy this car? What emotions does this ad appeal to?

The Craft of Advertising: Selling the Feeling

Hundreds of companies compete for our business, offering similar goods and services at similar prices. They use advertising to attract our attention, to make their products and services stand out from the competition, and to persuade us to buy.

An advertisment has four jobs. It must get people's **attention**, despite the hundreds of competing ads they see or hear every day. It must establish an **image** or personality for a product, creating associations or connections between that product and a need, desire, or an attractive lifestyle. It must **reassure** customers who have already bought the product or paid for the service that they have made the right choice, thus maintaining customer loyalty. And it must **persuade** new customers (often young people who have never tried the product or service before) that the product or service will benefit them in some way, frequently by appealing to the need for self-esteem.

advertising: the paid use of the media, such as television, radio, magazines, billboards, and newspapers, to bring a product or service to the attention of the people the advertiser wants to reach, with the goal of increasing sales

Activity

1. a) In a group, study a selection of current ads—from television, radio, newspapers, magazines, billboards, and public transit vehicles. If you cannot bring a copy of the ad to class, write a brief description of it. Then examine and compare the ads by discussing the questions raised in the following list. You might want to record your findings in chart form. Keep the ads and your notes in your media log for future use.
- Where and when does the ad appear?
- How many people appear in it? What is each person's age, gender, and race?
- How big is the print ad or how long is the TV or radio commercial?

- How many times is the name of the product mentioned?
- How much information is provided about the product?
- How often and how clearly do you see the product?
- What needs or emotions does the ad appeal to?
- How does it "hook" us (get our attention)?

b) Review the four jobs of advertising described on page 70. Choose four ads that perform each of the jobs described. Explain how they perform those jobs.

How to Produce Advertising that Sells

BY DAVID OGILVY

David Ogilvy is the founder of the fourth largest advertising agency in the world. In his books, he defends advertising as a business and tells readers how to succeed in the industry. In the following excerpts from Ogilvy on Advertising, *he gives his formula for successful advertising. Despite the passage of time since Ogilvy wrote this formula, his observations remain current and useful.*

You don't stand a tinker's chance of producing successful advertising unless you start by doing your homework. I have always found this extremely tedious, but there is no substitute for it.

First, study the product you are going to advertise. The more you know about it, the more likely you are to come up with a big idea for selling it. When I got the Rolls-Royce account, I spent three weeks reading about the car and came across a statement that "at sixty miles an hour, the loudest noise comes from the electric clock." This became the headline, and it was followed by 607 words of factual copy.

Your next chore is to find out what kind of advertising your competitors have been doing for similar products, and with what success. This will give you your bearings.

Now comes research among consumers. Find out how they think about your kind of product, what language they use when they discuss the subject, what attributes are important to them, *and what promise would be most likely to make them buy your brand.*

Positioning

Now consider how you want to "position" your product. This curious verb is in great favor among marketing experts, but no two of them agree on what it means. My own definition is "what the product does, and who it is for." I could have positioned Dove as a detergent bar for men with dirty hands, but chose instead to position it as a toilet bar for women with dry skin. This is still working 25 years later.

In Norway, the SAAB car had no measurable profile. We positioned it as a car for *winter*. Three years later it was voted the best car for Norwegian winters.

> **marketing:** *the process of promoting and selling a product or service based on decisions about what the product image should be and who is most likely to buy the product or service*

Brand Image

You now have to decide what "image" you want for your brand. Image means *personality*. Products, like people, have personalities, and they can make or break them in the market place. The personality of a product is an amalgam of many things—its name, its packaging, its price, the style of its advertising, and, above all, the nature of the product itself.

It pays to give most products an image of quality—*a First Class ticket*. This is particularly true of products whose brand-name is visible to your friends, like beer, cigarettes and automobiles: products you "wear." If your advertising looks cheap or shoddy, it will rub off on your product. Who wants to be seen using shoddy products?

Take whiskey. Why do some people choose Jack Daniel's, while others choose Grand Dad or Taylor? Have they tried all three and compared the taste? Don't make me laugh. The reality is that these three brands have different *images* which appeal to different kinds of people. It isn't the whiskey

they choose, it's the image. The brand image is 90 percent of what the distiller has to sell.

Writing advertising for any kind of liquor is an extremely subtle art. I once tried using rational facts to *argue* the consumer into choosing a brand of whiskey. It didn't work. You don't catch Coca-Cola advertising that Coke contains 30 percent more cola berries.

Next time an apostle of hard-sell questions the importance of brand images, ask him how Marlboro climbed from obscurity to become the biggest-selling cigarette in the world. Leo Burnett's cowboy campaign, started 25 years ago and continued to this day, has given the brand an image which appeals to smokers all over the world.

What's the big idea?

You can do homework from now until doomsday, but you will never win fame and fortune unless you also invent *big ideas*. It takes a big idea to attract the attention of consumers and get them to buy your product. Unless your advertising contains a big idea, it will pass like a ship in the night.

My partner Esty Stowell complained that the first commercial I wrote for Pepperidge Farm bread was sound enough, but lacking in imagery. That night I dreamed of two white horses pulling a baker's delivery van along a country lane at a smart trot. Today, 27 years later, that horse-drawn van is still driving up that lane in Pepperidge commercials.

When asked what was the best asset a person could have, Albert Lasker—the most astute of all advertising people—replied, "Humility in the presence of a

◄ One way to recognize a great idea is to ask if it could be used for 30 years, as this horse-drawn bakery van has been.

good idea." It is horribly difficult to *recognize* a good idea. I shudder to think how many I have rejected. Research can't help you much because it cannot predict the *cumulative* value of an idea, and no idea is big unless it will work for 30 years.

It will help you recognize a big idea if you ask yourself five questions:
1. Did it make me gasp when I first saw it?
2. Do I wish I had thought of it myself?
3. Is it unique?
4. Does it fit the strategy to perfection?
5. Could it be used for 30 years?

"The positively good"

A problem which confronts agencies is that so many products are no different from their competitors. Manufacturers have access to the same technology: marketing people use the same research procedures to determine consumer preferences for color, size, design, taste and so on. When faced with selling "parity" [similar] products, all you can hope to do is explain their virtues more persuasively than your competitors, and to differentiate them by the style of your advertising. This is the "added value" which advertising contributes, and I am not sufficiently puritanical to hate myself for it.

My partner Joel Raphaelson has articulated a feeling which has been growing in my mind for some time:

"In the past, just about every advertiser has assumed that in order to sell his goods he has to convince consumers that his product is *superior* to his competitor's.

"This may not be necessary. It may be sufficient to convince consumers that your product is *positively good*. If the consumer feels certain that your product is good and feels uncertain about your competitor's, he will buy yours.

This approach to advertising parity products does not insult the intelligence of consumers. Who can blame you for putting your best foot forward?

—Ogilvy on Advertising, 1983

See also Video 2, Excerpts 21 & 22.

1. In groups, examine a few ads from the ones you collected for Activity 1 on page 70, and decide how closely they follow David Ogilvy's advice for good advertising. Consider the target markets of the ads, the images the ads create, and ways you think the advertisers might have improved their campaigns. Present your conclusions to the class.

2. In groups, use the list of five questions on page 73 that help to recognize a "big idea" in advertising to discuss some recent ad campaigns. You might consider campaigns for fast-food restaurants, soft drinks, batteries, beer, cars, or jeans. Which campaigns would you rate as "big ideas"? Present your choices to the class with your reasons for choosing them. How many of your classmates agree with you?

3. Follow the process Ogilvy described for producing successful advertising, starting with research and ending with "the big idea," and plan an ad campaign. You might choose to advertise a favourite product, such as a soft drink or brand of running shoes, or a service you use frequently, such as a fast-food restaurant, sports club, or library. Create or videotape one ad and present it to the class.

Psychographics

BY WILLIAM MEYERS

Researchers have discovered that magazine readers spend little more than two seconds glancing over a page. On TV, a typical commercial "spot" is only 15- or 30-seconds long, and many viewers "flip" or "channel surf" through commercial breaks. In order to connect quickly with today's consumers, advertisers often create strong emotional appeals based on "psychographics," an analysis of people's attitudes, beliefs, desires, and needs. Although a creative team cannot predict how each individual will react to a campaign, psychographics gives them a good idea of how large groups within the population will react. As you read the following article about one psychographic approach called VALS (Values and Life-Styles), consider how you feel about the approach and the assumptions it makes. Try to determine to which group(s) you and people you know belong.

The world according to VALS is simple. There are essentially five basic groups of citizens—Belongers, Emulators, Emulator-Achievers, Societally Conscious Achievers, and the Need-Directed.

VALS tells us that almost one out of three citizens in the United States is a *Belonger*—the typical traditionalist, the cautious and conforming conservative. The Belonger believes in God, country, and family. The lifeblood of the Belonger's world is a strong community consciousness. Change is his or her arch-enemy. Without a secure, stable, and structured society, this staunch defender of the status quo is unable to cope.

VOICE-OVER: Both mother and daughter believe that a car saved their lives that day.

VOLVO
Drive Safely

▲ Which of the VALS groups would this ad most appeal to?

The Belonger's consumer profile reflects his old-fashioned view of things. He usually drives a Dodge or a Plymouth; he drinks Coke, Pepsi, or Budweiser; he eats at McDonald's with the family; he loves Jell-O.

Emulators are not so set in their ways. They are a small but impressionable group of young people in desperate search of an identity and a place in the adult working world. These kids, who represent about 15 percent of the American population, will do almost anything to fit in. Most of them lack self-confidence and are discouraged about their prospects. They envision little future for themselves in our society. They compensate for this pessimism with unabashed personal hedonism. Confused and vulnerable, Emulators will purchase products from advertisers who offer solutions to their postadolescent dilemmas. In dealing with Emulators, advertisers prey on their insecurity.

Chevrolet, for example, has sold hundreds of thousands of Camaros to these uncertain youngsters by positioning the vehicle as the coolest car on the market.

Emulator-Achievers, America's materialists, have already made it. These acquisitive consumers often own a Mercedes; they feel most comfortable with such "uptown" brand names as Dom Perignon, Tiffany, or Gucci; and they have to have the latest in high-tech toys. But Emulator-Achievers, approximately 20 percent of the population, are in a funk. Once they believed the sky was the limit; today they feel frustrated, perhaps a bit cheated, stuck just below the top rung of the economic ladder. Despite their relative affluence, three quarters of them fear they won't be able to attain their fiscal goals during the coming decade.

Madison Avenue cheers up Emulator-Achievers with commercials that transform everyday items into accoutrements of accomplishment, success, and taste. Advertisers convince these compulsive consumers that by purchasing certain products they will be seen as the modern aristocrats they seek to be.

Societally Conscious Achievers are the flower children of America's consumer culture. They care more about inner peace and environmental safety than about financial success and elegant surroundings. Personal, not professional, fulfillment matters most to these individualists. Societally Conscious Achievers, constituting approximately 20 percent of the U.S. population, are experimental—they will try anything from acupuncture to Zen, as long as it fits into their uncomplicated life-style. Many of them are dropouts from the world of commerce —reformed strivers who no longer see the need for conspicuous consumption.

Societally Conscious Achievers often shop for their clothing by mail, choosing L.L. Bean moccasins over Gucci loafers, and they usually drive small foreign cars—Mazda, Honda, Volvo, or Subaru. Lighter wines or such wholesome beverages as herbal tea, fruit juice, or bottled water are preferred by these inner-directed citizens.

Need-Directed Americans are the survivors, the people struggling to sustain themselves on subsistence incomes. Mostly welfare recipients, Social Security beneficiaries, and minimum-wage earners, these citizens, who represent close to 15 percent of the country, aren't consumers in the true sense of the word. They're so busy trying to make ends meet that they don't really have time to worry about the type of beer they drink or the image projected by the cigarettes they smoke. The Need-Directed aren't driving new cars or acquiring state-of-the-art personal computers, and they rarely have enough money to take the family out for even a fast-food meal.

—*The Image-Makers*, 1984

See also Video 1, Excerpt 9.

Activities

1. **a)** Jot down the names of some characters in popular TV shows who would fit into each of the four groups.
   b) How useful do you think VALS would be in identifying potential consumers for a product?

2. **a)** In your media log, describe the members of your family or some of your friends and decide which VALS group each person belongs to. Many people fit into more than one group.
   b) How do you feel about slotting people into groups such as these?

3. With a group, survey newspapers and magazines to collect a number of ads that you think will appeal to each of the VALS groups. Discuss your findings with another group or the class.

4. In groups, choose one of the following products—a breakfast cereal, a soft drink, a car, a watch, or a product of your choice—and create an ad that appeals to one of the four VALS groups. Show your ad to the class and have them guess which group your ad has been created for.

See also
Resource Binder
page 44.

Constructing Emotional Appeal

Once advertisers have chosen their target markets, they have eight main elements or ingredients to use for constructing an ad that speaks to the heart. These eight elements are: models, setting, copy, sound, story, colour, point of view, and details. Look at the diagram below and consider how these elements have been used to construct the emotional appeal in the McDonald's ad that appears on the next page. Since this is a print ad, the advertisers used only seven of the eight elements.

As with any media text, there are many ways of reading the ad. We have provided a fictional account of how a creative team might have interpreted this ad for a McDonald's marketing manager. As you read the account, consider whether or not you agree with this interpretation. How else might you interpret it?

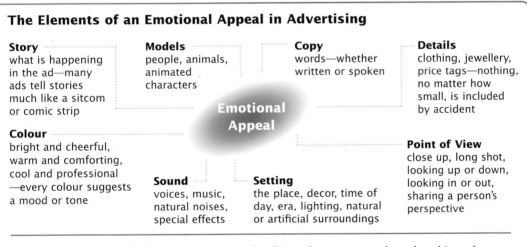

The Elements of an Emotional Appeal in Advertising

Story
what is happening in the ad—many ads tell stories much like a sitcom or comic strip

Models
people, animals, animated characters

Copy
words—whether written or spoken

Details
clothing, jewellery, price tags—nothing, no matter how small, is included by accident

Colour
bright and cheerful, warm and comforting, cool and professional —every colour suggests a mood or tone

Emotional Appeal

Sound
voices, music, natural noises, special effects

Setting
the place, decor, time of day, era, lighting, natural or artificial surroundings

Point of View
close up, long shot, looking up or down, looking in or out, sharing a person's perspective

Although every individual responds to an ad in his or her own way, based on his or her experiences and attitudes, advertisers carefully build each ad to create a specific emotional appeal. Through research and experience, advertisers can predict fairly accurately how large groups of people will respond to a campaign.

What You Give Is What You Get

Models We have four people in the ad: an attractive young couple with one child, and a grandmother. They are all well dressed, suggesting financial stability. Associating the McDonald's name with this family suggests that McDonald's cares about "family values," while showing that the products appeal to all ages.

Setting We've set the ad in a house in an anonymous town or city. The winter weather is the first hint of Christmas. As you can see, there is a car outside, full-length drapes at the window, and an attractive carpet on the floor. All these elements reinforce the middle-class image of the family.

Details We've put the older woman in a wheelchair so that McDonald's can be seen to acknowledge the needs of the disabled. We've made her look quite grandmotherly, with her thick sweater and the book on her lap. But we've spiced the image up a bit with the jewellery, nail polish, and dress shoes.

Story Our ad tells the story of a surprise visit to grandmother, a woman who could not travel easily in the winter. Her visitors have picked up some McDonald's take-out so that she won't have to cook. The grandmother's hand position is a code for surprise: you can almost hear her saying, "Oh my!" as she sees her family arrive.

Copy "Holiday spirit," "spirit of the season," and "giving" all suggest the Christmas season, but we've avoided references that exclude anyone who doesn't celebrate Christmas. We've made no specific reference to any McDonald's product. Instead, we thought the Christmas season would be a good time to build McDonald's image as a company that cares about families.

Point of View We've placed the camera in the room with the grandmother so the audience will share her pleasure at seeing the family outside. That feeling of pleasure and welcome will then colour the audience's response to the McDonald's logo on the bags the family carries.

Colour We've used warm, bright colours to give the ad a happy feel. The warm wood of the window frame stands out nicely against the cold snow and draws attention to the visiting family. And notice that the red coat on the woman matches the colour of the McDonald's logo on the bags and in the lower right-hand corner of the ad.

What You Give Is What You Get...

When we give from the heart, we share in the true holiday spirit. Here's wishing you and your family the spirit of the season all year long.

What you want is what you get...*Guaranteed.*

McDonald's

MUSIC: to set mood; jazzy,
no lyrics

MUSIC: cont'd
SFX: car engine (quietly)

MUSIC: cont'd
SFX: tires on wet pavement

MUSIC: cont'd

MUSIC: chorus joins in

MUSIC: cont'd

MUSIC: female soloist
joins in
LYRICS: "Tried, tested..."

MUSIC: cont'd
LYRICS: "...and true..."

MUSIC: slows for finale
LYRICS: "...I know that you'll
always come through."

▲ What does the element of sound add to the emotional appeal of this TV ad?

In the McDonald's ad, the product appears as a "natural" part of the setting. In ads that appeal to the emotions, the product may not appear at all, or may not be identified specifically, except as a logo or voice-over. Look at the TV ad above and examine how the elements of an emotional appeal are used.

Activities

1. In a small group, collect a few recent ads and describe the emotional appeal in each. Consider how The Elements of an Emotional Appeal on page 77 were used to create the overall effect.

2. **a)** Find one print ad that appeals to each of the following emotional needs: friendship and acceptance; a warm and loving family; admiration and self-esteem; physical attractiveness.

**See also Video 2,
Excerpts 19 & 20.**

b) Examine how The Elements of an Emotional Appeal identified in the diagram on page 77 were used in each ad.

c) Explain how some of these ads appeal to more than one basic need at a time.

3. Select a variety of ads with slogans or catchy phrases. Examine the words and phrases used to see how they help to create the product image. Here are some examples of successful slogans.
"Built for the human race" — *Nissan automobiles*
"Reebok lets U be U" — *Reebok shoes*
"Just Do It" — *Nike shoes*

Fashion Trends

probe

Who sets fashion trends? The fashion business is so large and so international that many of the decisions about what is "in" and what will be for sale in the stores near you are made thousands of miles away. Since most popular clothing stores are part of national or international retail chains, the fashions they sell are part of nation-wide or world-wide marketing strategies.

How do you find out about fashion trends? From your friends? Popular TV shows? Favourite musicians? Fashion magazines? Your own taste? Fashion ads?

Controversial Ads

Today, we are surrounded by more and better advertising than ever before. It is more difficult for an ad to stand out from the crowd and capture our attention. Some advertisers have chosen to win the public's attention by using ads that shock.

Some ads create shock value by using sexually-suggestive images of nearly nude models posed in provocative positions.

See also page 48.

Makers of cosmetics, perfumes, and fashions, especially jeans, have used this type of ad successfully for years. Think of ads you have seen for Calvin Klein, Hollywood, or Guess jeans.

Other advertisers centre their campaigns on social issues, such as racial intolerance, violence, or war. Benetton, a European clothing manufacturer, created global advertising campaigns for magazines and billboards using images such as a man dying of AIDS or refugees swarming on an already overloaded ship. Oliviero Toscani, who created the Benetton ads, claimed these campaigns were intended as social criticism. Many of Benetton's critics claimed they only exploited misery and suffering to sell clothes.

Both kinds of controversial ads, those that raise issues and those that are simply provocative, succeed at one thing: they grab the attention of the buying public. They also attract complaints and boycotts from consumer groups. But whether people like these ads or hate them, they are likely to remember them, and that can make them successful for the advertisers, despite any complaints.

**See also
Resource Binder
page 45.**

"If someone from another planet visited the Earth in a few hundred years and judged from the advertisements, he'd think our life consisted of idyllic families and luxury goods. But the real world grapples with terrible problems such as AIDS, racism, discrimination against those who are different, ecological disasters and wars. I introduce these problems into advertising."

—Oliviero Toscani in the *Toronto Star*, August 20, 1995

Activities

1. a) What do you think of the ads reproduced here and on p. 82? Do you find them shocking or controversial? Why or why not? What messages do they convey?

b) Think of another ad you have found shocking or controversial. In your media log, describe the ad and explain why it bothered you.

c) Who benefits when advertisers use controversial issues and images in their advertising? Explain.

**See also
page 15.**

◀ Diesel Jeans uses unusual visual images to challenge viewers about issues such as wearing fur.

See also Video 1, Excerpts 1 & 13.

2. Gather some examples of cosmetic and fashion ads and use them to debate the following: Advertisers should be free to use sexually-suggestive images in advertising.

3. With a group, list some benefits and drawbacks to controversial advertising. Then decide whether or not you would use controversial ads to promote each of the following: clothing, cars, and headache pills. Consider who you want to sell your product to and the image you wish to create for it.

Advertising in Your School

In recent years, advertising and marketing activities have been moving into schools. Until recently, schools have either been ignored by marketers or considered off-limits to marketing campaigns. Although in the past some companies have donated maps or bookcovers to schools, only products and activities related to school life such as school rings, yearbooks, and graduation photographs were advertised on school property.

But today, there are many companies and institutions, including governments, who have messages to convey to students and they are using various forms of advertising to send those messages. Examine the diagram on the next page to see the variety of marketing messages aimed at students. Then find out what kind of advertising exists in your school. Investigate such areas as the main office, student services, classrooms, the cafeteria, and the gym. Record all the examples of advertising and promotion you find, using the chart on page 84 of the Resource Binder.

Activities

1. **a)** What types of messages do the examples of advertising in your school communicate?
   b) How effective are these examples of advertising? To help you evaluate them, use The Elements of an Emotional Appeal in Advertising on page 77 of this chapter and A Guide to Deconstructing a Visual on page 105 of the Resource Binder.

2. To reach adolescent audiences, some agencies design ads for schools that might be considered controversial. These ads usually relate to issues of public health and safety. Can you find examples of such ads in your school? Are they effective? Do students consider them controversial? Do parents?

Who's Selling What?
The following are major sources of promotional messages affecting values, attitudes, and lifestyle choices.

Federal, Provincial, and Municipal Governments
Goal: to win public support for policies and programs

Producers and Sellers of Consumer Products
Goal: to win the loyalty of young consumers

Universities and Colleges
Goal: to influence teens' decisions about higher education

Corporate Public Relations Departments
Goal: to foster goodwill and public support for business and industries

YOU

TV Networks, Movie and Music Producers and Promoters
Goal: to attract audiences ready to buy the products of advertisers and sponsors

Sports and Recreation Organizations
Goal: to attract young, active members with money and time to spend

School Boards and Departments of Education
Goal: to encourage adherence to school rules and continued attendance

Health Care and Service Organizations
Goal: to promote healthy and safe lifestyles and responsible citizenship

Students earn and spend their own money and face many important lifestyle decisions. Many businesses and institutions go to great lengths to influence those decisions and spending choices.

Selling Lifestyles in Schools

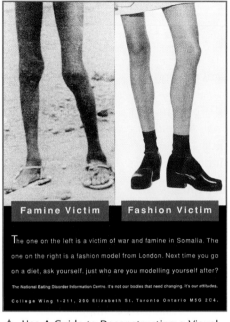

Famine Victim   **Fashion Victim**

The one on the left is a victim of war and famine in Somalia. The one on the right is a fashion model from London. Next time you go on a diet, ask yourself, just who are you modelling yourself after?

The National Eating Disorder Information Centre. It's not our bodies that need changing. It's our attitudes.

College Wing 1-211, 200 Elizabeth St. Toronto Ontario M5G 2C4.

▲ Use A Guide to Deconstructing a Visual on page 105 of the Resource Binder to analyze the message in this poster.

Advertising is a powerful medium of communication, so it is often used to promote ideas as well as products. Governments and health organizations work together with school authorities to promote healthy and positive lifestyles: these campaigns may include anti-smoking, anti-drinking, and anti-drug messages. There are also anti-racism and anti-sexism campaigns that promote tolerance, understanding, and respect for people's differences.

Schools also promote safety through safe walking and cycling lessons, driver's education classes, and conflict-resolution training. Many schools also have serious penalties for violence. School versions of Crime Stoppers and Neighbourhood Watch encourage students to report criminal activity. Because these programs allow anonymous reports, they guard students against reprisals for "telling." These campaigns try to show that violence is more than just illegal: it is also unattractive and unacceptable.

Schools promote health and safety campaigns according to the needs of the community. In some schools, an AIDS awareness campaign may only generate a few posters on the wall, while in others, the campaign may involve students in special projects and school-wide assemblies.

Activities

1. How many different health and safety campaigns are being promoted at your school? Which do you think is the most effective? Why? Identify the organizations who sponsor these campaigns and suggest why they do so.

2. a) Describe the lifestyle suggested by the health and safety campaigns and rules of conduct at your school.
b) Describe the lifestyle portrayed in a typical ad, a favourite TV program, or the words to your favourite song.
c) Compare the lifestyles described in a) and b) above. Which is more attractive to you? Which is more attainable? Explain.

See also page 27.

Future Educational Choices

Today, most colleges and universities use inviting and colourful posters to attract students. A typical poster will include a colour photograph of a beautiful outdoor campus scene, showing off the physical setting of the school. Front and centre in this scene will be a group of young, attractive, and friendly student models from a variety of ethnic backgrounds. Like the advertisements that market soft drinks and beer to the same age group, the posters promote friendship and good times in an attractive setting. The copy is frequently limited to the name of the institution, or may include a snappy slogan, such as "The New U." or "The choice is yours." Most posters offer no real information about the programs offered by the college or university, or its admission requirements. Instead, they concentrate on selling a positive image.

Other posters may use eye-catching or unusual visuals to construct a particular product image for the school. The visual may be anything from a computer-manipulated image suggesting an up-to-date, fresh approach to education, to a well-known historical figure suggesting the strength and stability of tradition.

In the hot competition for students, colleges and universities have learned to apply valuable lessons from the world of commercial advertising. The traditional elitist image of ivy-covered universities has been replaced with new images that appeal to students' emotional needs and desires.

▲ Which school would you choose? Why?

Activities

1. Analyze the university and college posters displayed in your own school, or reproduced here, by responding to the following questions:
   - If students are shown, what do they look like? What are they doing? What impression do they give you of the school they represent? Are they real students or models?
   - If students do not appear, what image was chosen and what does it say about the institution?

See also
page 77.

- What are the emotional appeals in each of the posters? What elements were used to create these appeals?
- How effective are the slogans that the various schools use? Choose those you like best and least, and explain your choices.
- What overall "image" of the school does each poster suggest to you?

2. Choose one poster for a college or university and one ad for a product such as running shoes, soft drinks, or jeans and compare them. Consider the visual images, the copy, and the emotional appeals in the ads. What similarities and differences are there between them?

3. In groups or as a class, debate the following: Improved advertising for colleges and universities will help to improve post-secondary education in Canada.

Corporate Sponsorship in Schools

Corporate sponsorship in schools has generated a great deal of controversy. It has been described as exploitation of a "captive audience." Students are required to attend school by law and therefore don't have much freedom of choice when a direct marketing message is delivered there. But supporters of corporate sponsorship point out that in tight economic times, sponsorships pay for activities that schools otherwise couldn't afford.

corporate sponsorship: providing money, products, or services to an organization or group to support their programs or events and to generate positive publicity for the sponsor

See also
Resource Binder
page 47.

As tempting as corporate funding may sound, many educators are cautious when offered sponsorship deals. They recognize that companies and products may take on added significance when promoted at school. Corporate sponsorship may provide needed funds, but these funds come with a price.

What kind of message does the presence of corporate sponsorship in schools send to students? What impact do corporate sponsors have on how teachers teach and what students learn? What are the long-term consequences of sponsorship programs? These are some of the questions to keep in mind as you read the following two articles about businesses that offer to help schools finance their programs—in return for some effective promotion.

Educating the Market

BY JAMES POLLOCK

As far as high school principals go, Art Kelly at Assumption Catholic Secondary School in Burlington, Ont., just may be the best friend a marketer ever had. He's also got some ideas that his students like, too. Just before a class change, for example, he might go on the P.A. system to announce that Coca-Cola Bottling has donated some concert tickets, and that there will be a draw in the auditorium to determine who gets them.

Kelly says "bunk" to the idea that commercial messages and interests have no place in schools, and points to a detailed list of benefits that may not otherwise be available. For example, in a hard-fought tendering process with rival Pepsi to decide who would supply all the school's soft drinks, Coke sweetened its offer with many perks for the classroom. Beyond the pop and the draws for prizes, Coke said it would provide managers to speak at business classes, distribute videos and other instructional materials, give away T-shirts for fundraising events, sponsor the school's Terry Fox charity walk, and donate a $400 "Assumption School" sign. In this day and economic age, Kelly believes he has to have an eye for a good deal. "People have to realize we're in the '90s now, and the idea of running a 'pure' school with four walls and a teacher with a piece of chalk is gone," he says. "The public doesn't want their taxes to go up. Where else are we going to get the money?"

Kelly is certainly not alone in arguing the need to link commerce with education. Marketers recognize the value of access to thousands and thousands of growing consumers. Hard pressed for money to fund programs, the schools and school boards themselves are turning more to companies as potential sources of revenue.

In the Calgary area, Rocky View School Division No. 41 has approved placing advertisements on its 160 school buses. The only thing the board needs to decide is what kind of ads will be allowed, says Darrell Couture, secretary-treasurer. Anything highly controversial will probably be disallowed, from condom ads to "perhaps jean ads, for example, if they show a scantily-clad girl," he says.

Indeed, even the general idea of making an alliance between commerce and the school system makes some people uncomfortable. Last year, when the Toronto School Board signed a three-year, $1.14 million contract with Pepsi-Cola Canada to help subsidize its food services operation, some members of the public were highly critical. Even some of the students protested, saying they were being denied free choice and that they were pawns of big business. In an editorial (Jan. 31, 1994), this magazine took the line that "students should not be treated as a target audience to be bartered off to the highest bidder, especially by those charged with safeguarding the quality of their education."

These days, however, there does seem to be an aggressiveness on both sides to forge alliances between schools and businesses. Margot Swindall, formerly with Toronto food supply firm Restauronics, says food suppliers that want to maintain

"There is an obvious reason for business's rising interest in education. Marketing firms like Griffin Bacal Volny and Creative Children's Marketing describe children as the new 'hot' target market. According to a recent StatsCan study, children aged 2–12 spend $1.5 billion each year, and influence another $15 billion. Total spending per year for 13–24 year olds is $7.8 billion, according to The Globe and Mail (Classroom Edition), *and this is a market business feels it cannot ignore."*

—Erika Shaker, *Education Forum*, Fall 1995

their school contracts often have to sweeten their offerings. When she worked at Restauronics, almost every bid she saw going out to schools had such extras attached as money for scholarship programs. The competition to provide goods and services to the school system is so intense that suppliers can't just think in terms of basic service.

Paul Glover, vice-president of campus services for Toronto-based Versa Services Ltd., says campus sales have grown 500% since 1982, the brunt of that realized in the last three years. Contracts with other food vendors, such as setting up Mr. Submarine carts in cafeterias, are helping to drive that growth. "Just about everybody is coming to us—frozen yogurt, pizza, tacos."

Some firms have looked to increase their presence by linking their products more intimately with the whole purpose of the school system. The Ontario Milk Marketing Board moved to gear up its high-school program, in part by relying less on its own sales reps and more on joint programs with food service operators. Also, next September, it will launch computer-based curriculum units that refer to milk.

"For a class unit on processes and production, say, we could provide a whole unit showing how milk is produced," says Nick Price-Owen, assistant director of the product promotion division of the Mississauga, Ont.-based marketing board. "Sampling, heavy branding are considered exploitation. But partnerships with schools that help their curriculum needs are not."

Burlington principal Art Kelly can point to important non-monetary payoffs for the kind of commercial deals he's made, too. He believes companies can enrich school life, whether it's through the work experience provided by Westinghouse in its co-op work program or through the deal that has Coca-Cola donating some concert tickets. In the prize draws, both student and teacher names are thrown into the hat, and the implicit message is that the school community works as a team. "There's little graffiti at our school and the flowerbeds aren't destroyed," he says. "If they were, it would be bye-bye to the Rolling Stones concert tickets."

—*Marketing Magazine*, January 2, 1995

1. List several examples of sponsorship and promotion mentioned in the article. How many of these examples were on your list from the survey of advertising in your own school (page 82)?

2. There is a lot of controversy over corporate sponsorship in schools. Where would you draw the line? In your media log, describe the kind of sponsorship agreements you think would be acceptable. Which ones do you think would be exploitive?

3. What values are suggested to the Burlington students through the rewards made possible by their school's sponsors? Do you think these are values schools ought to support? Explain your answer.

Schools Go Commercial

BY MICHAEL F. JACOBSON AND LAURIE ANN MAZUR

Although the examples in the following article are American, several of the companies mentioned are also approaching Canadian schools. As you read, consider the advantages and disadvantages of these sponsorship arrangements.

PORT ANGELES, WASHINGTON. It's Mary Leinart's first day in sixth grade. As she nervously takes her seat in homeroom class, a TV monitor blinks on. A few announcements, then with a blast of loud rock music and dazzling graphics, Channel One fills the screen. For the next twelve minutes, Mary and her classmates watch a frenetically paced amalgam of hard news (wars, elections, a solar eclipse) and human interest stories (dating, high school sports) punctuated by two minutes worth of ads for sneakers, junk food, and other products. Sometimes it's hard to tell the ads from the rest of the program: A music review, for example, openly plugs the latest albums by heavy metal bands Megadeth, Slayer, and Anthrax.

Welcome, Mary, to public education in the 1990s, where advertisements fill the hallways and classrooms and ooze their way into the curriculum.

Thousands of American corporations provide curricular and other material for schools, often through marketing companies such as Lifetime Learning Systems of Fairfield, Connecticut. "Let Lifetime Learning Systems bring your message to the classroom, where young people are forming attitudes that will last a lifetime," purrs the company's sales kit, "Whatever your objective, we can help you meet it." Hundreds of

companies and other entities have hired Lifetime to peddle their wares (or ideologies) in the schools, including the American Nuclear Society, Coca-Cola Company, the National Frozen Pizza Institute, the Snack Food Association, and the government of Saudi Arabia. Lifetime claims to reach 63 million young people every year.

> *"Corporate sponsorship is disastrous for a democracy. Sponsorship is the worst possible mechanism for distributing resources in any culture or society. It gives the most to those who need it the least because sponsors want to be associated with already proven success."*
> —Len Masterman, media critic in *Mediacy*, Spring 1995

Lifetime is up front about using the authority of the classroom to benefit advertisers. "Coming from school," promises the sales kit, "all these materials carry an extra measure of credibility that gives your message added weight." Another ad asks potential clients to "IMAGINE millions of students discussing your product in class. IMAGINE their teachers presenting your organization's point of view."

Although Lifetime's promotional literature declares that its materials "combine both strong commercial appeal and sound educational information," the educational value of its curricula is highly suspect. For example, one Lifetime teaching kit, entitled *Count Your Chips*, is sponsored by the National Potato Board and the Snack Food Association. Its first activity urges kids to "be a chip-e-matician!" by digesting facts about potato chips and solving simple math problems. Students are told that "each person in the United States eats about six pounds of potato chips in one year" and are asked to calculate the number of one-ounce bags of chips that represents.

Companies are training students to support industry in contemporary policy debates. Mobil hired Learning Enrichment Inc. to produce a series called *Critical Thinking About Critical Issues 92-93*. One unit in the series addressed the debate surrounding the North American Free Trade Agreement (NAFTA), which Mobil staunchly supported. The curriculum included a published Mobil editorial on the virtues of NAFTA, with no discussion of the company's commercial bias. The subsequent "questions for a critical thinker" were designed to help the student understand and support the conclusion of the Mobil editorial, not to question it.

Increasingly, schools are entering into full-fledged partnerships with business. These partnerships can take many forms, including on-the-job training or corporate-sponsored skill-building programs.

So what's wrong with corporate-school partnerships? A lot, says Alex Molnar, a professor of education at the University of Wisconsin at Milwaukee who has studied commercialism in schools. "Business and schools do *not* have the same interests—despite what business says. A business's first responsibility is to the people who own it. That usually means making the largest profit as quickly as possible. In contrast, public schools belong to us all and exist to promote the public welfare."

Corporate interest in schools is one-dimensional: Companies want to sell products and services. But the public schools have a broader mandate to produce citizens who can think critically and participate in democracy. That includes thinking critically about the advertising messages they are bombarded with daily. In a school where the content and form of education is influenced by advertisers, will students be encouraged to question the means and motivations of business? Will the information that companies want to impart squeeze out more important information?

—*Marketing Madness, A Survival Guide for a Consumer Society*, 1995

Activities

1. Critics of corporate sponsorship in schools claim that one goal of such agreements is to develop buying habits in students.

a) What do companies do to develop consumer habits or brand loyalties among students?

b) How do you think corporate sponsorship will influence students' decisions about what they buy? Give examples.

2. In small groups, reread the last two paragraphs of the article, then respond to the following question. Present your conclusions to the class.

- In what ways might sponsorship arrangements affect students' abilities to think critically about advertising and the methods and ideology of business?

3. a) Do you think educators should allow businesses to bring marketing messages to students in the schools? Why or why not? Record your thoughts in your media log.

b) Read the Guidelines for Partnerships in Education on page 85 of the Resource Binder, then write a letter to your local school trustee expressing your thoughts about the role of corporate sponsorship in schools.

Beyond Advertising: The World of Public Relations

media

probe

A Day in the Life...

You wake up to the sound of this week's number one, top-of-the-charts tune. The new clock radio that you got free when you subscribed to *Teen Generation* magazine sure beats the old alarm! While eating breakfast, you catch a special news feature on nutrition. It gives you some excellent information for your health project. Since it's produced by the Milk Marketing Board, the information must be reliable.

At school, you're pleased to hear that first period is cancelled. Instead, the whole school is going to the auditorium to see a shocking new play on teen violence, generously funded by Mobile Alarm Systems. In second period, you go to the library and work on the new computerized weather program, donated to your school by Hardrive Canada. While doing research on the nation's weather patterns, you find an encouraging press release from the Ministry of the Environment and McMall Pulp and Paper on new growth in B.C.'s rainforests.

At lunch, you relax with your friends over a Burger Queen Special from one of the new vending booths in your caf and discuss your favorite topic—music! Rap's Bad Boys have just adopted a new clean-cut image. You can finally bring their CD home without getting in a big hassle with your parents! As soon as the 3:15 bell goes, you grab the bus to The Music Box to make your purchase.

— Why do companies pay for programs and giveaways like the ones described above and in the cartoon?

— In your media log, list as many examples of public relations promotions or events as you can. Describe one you were personally involved in. How did the event affect your impression of the business or institution that sponsored it?

Walnut Cove

The Sponsored Society

Business and governments care as much about their image as do most people. A positive image helps to inspire consumer confidence and public approval. These institutions pay for advertising to promote their products and services, but they run public relations programs to promote positive images of their organizations. Public relations programs may include sponsored special events such as open houses, picnics, fund-raisers, and news conferences. They also include charitable donations, information brochures, and public service-style ads. Ideally, these programs also receive free news coverage, which provides much more credible promotion than advertising can.

Organizations run regular public relations programs all year round, but they rely most heavily on public relations techniques during a crisis. When something goes wrong, such as a toxic spill or an accusation of illegal behaviour, a well-run public relations program draws attention to any good news while downplaying the bad news.

public relations (PR): the efforts and activities of a business, institution, or government to promote goodwill between itself and the public, and to create and maintain a positive public image

▲ Citgo, a petroleum company, is one of the sponsors of the Boston Marathon.

◀ What does this ad say about the LCBO?

Do you need a better reason?

LCBO PLEASE DRINK RESPONSIBLY.

Getting to know the
Esso Kids Program

Putting our energies to work for
Canada's kids and Canada's future.

▲ Why would Esso choose to run a kids'
program?

*"Practising good public relations means
researching and analyzing your reputation with the public, then planning and
executing specific programs to enhance or
improve that relationship. A wisely
planned PR program can build confidence
in a company's objectives and create a
receptive and favourable state of mind in
the public. The time to make friends is
before you need them."*
—Ruth Hammond, *Public Relations For
Small Business*, 1979

Activities

1. a) Read the quotation about public relations
above, then examine the ad, brochure, and
photograph on pages 93 and 94. How do
each of these public relations products enhance the image of the business or institution named in it?

b) Why would these
businesses and insti-
tutions choose to have
their names associated
with these messages
or events?

See also Resource
Binder page 49.

c) In what ways are these public relations
programs different from most advertising?

2. Imagine that you are the public relations manager for a business or institution that needs to improve its image. You might
choose to represent your own school, a local business or industry, or a sports team.

- Recommend a charity or community project for your client
to sponsor in order to improve its image and inspire confidence in the community. Explain how your recommendation
would affect your client's image.

- Prepare a promotional poster or brochure that highlights
your organization's charitable involvement.

**See also Video 4,
Excerpt 30.**

Fake News

BY DAVID LIEBERMAN

Public relations is used not only to make the public aware of a product or company, but also to make the product or company seem trustworthy. As one public relations executive explains, "Credibility is ultra-important. Advertising provides name ID. Editorial coverage provides credibility." Editorial coverage includes news stories and columns or commentaries prepared by journalists. This type of coverage is the ideal form of public relations because the news is more trusted than most other forms of media. But this style of public relations has disturbing implications for consumers, journalists, and the news industry. The following excerpts from a TV Guide *article describe how public relations programs can receive editorial coverage on television news.*

The *CBS Evening News* appeared to have put a lot of work into its June 13, 1991 segment on the hazards of automatic safety belts. The shoulder straps, announced correspondent Mark Phillips, are "a labor-saving device that may be costing lives instead of saving them." Proof: videotape of a car being tipped on its side, the door opening and the strap allowing a dummy to fall out and be crushed beneath the car.

A good piece, apparently showing the lengths to which CBS News would go to verify a report.

Trouble is, the videotape was not by CBS. Not that you'd have known it from the newscast; CBS's famous "eye" logo ran throughout the piece and there was no indication to the viewer as to who performed the demonstration. In fact, the tape was part of a "video news release" created by the Institute for Injury Reduction (IIR), a swell-sounding name for a lobby group largely supported by lawyers whose clients often sue auto companies for crash-related injuries. Indeed, say the group's opponents, IIR lawyers often show reports like the CBS segment in court to win cases, increase their clients' payments and fatten their fees. After all, juries find reports aired by CBS more credible than, say, some taped test by a group with an obvious ax to grind.

Score another hit for the fast-growing world of fake news.

Fake? Yes, to viewers who think of news as the work of independent journalists who broadcast their own reporting and camera work. But that's not what we see when reporters air the handiwork of PR firms out to plug a product, polish an image, or ensure that a particular political spin is spun.

Over the last few years, fake news has grown into a big business. Every day, PR pros supply the country's 700-plus local TV outlets and the national networks with news-like reports and features. In some cases, they offer stations prepaid

the Los Angeles Kings pays him for playing, push his annual income to an estimated $23.5 million. "Gretzky's legend has transcended his sport so that even mainstream American companies have been able to use him," says Jeff Jensen, who covers sports marketing for *Advertising Age*, the Chicago-based trade journal. "People know what he stands for even if they know nothing about hockey."

Gretzky has kept his business affairs mostly to himself—he hardly needs more publicity, and besides, it is *his* business. But what he once jokingly referred to as "my little empire" has become difficult to ignore. He has starred in major television advertising campaigns for such consumer giants as Domino's Pizza and Sharp Electronics. He is a corporate spokesman for Coca-Cola, Campbell Soup Co., and Zurich Insurance. He has boosted the bottom-line fortunes of such smaller companies as Easton Sports and in-line skate-maker First Team Sports. His name and image are licensed on dozens of products, from trading cards and posters to T-shirts and collectible plates. He has one restaurant in Toronto and has helped launch a North American chain of sports-themed restaurants in an all-star partnership that includes gridiron hero Joe Montana, tennis ace Andre Agassi and basketball behemoth Shaquille O'Neal. Time Warner, the giant U.S. communications firm, has designed an interactive video game around him, and he is spearheading a plan to build privately financed, family-oriented ice rinks across North America. "We have tried to build something I can fall back on

when I retire, something I can do when I finish playing hockey," he says.

He excites advertisers not so much for the records he sets as for the manner in which he sets them. He has a style all his own—signature moves inside an opponent's blue-line that give him space to shoot or to set up a teammate in the clear. He is creative, finding scoring opportunities from seeming chaos. He is a team player, whose assist totals are even more remarkable than his goal records. And he is generous, reflecting glory on teammates, past players and the greatness of the game.

Clean-living and clean-cut, he is a model citizen off the ice as well. Advertisers cringe when their walking billboards attract negative publicity: examples range from the relatively benign, such as figure skater Nancy Kerrigan's post-Olympics petulance, to the more serious—golfer John Daly's alcoholism, sprinter Ben Johnson's steroid scandals and, of course, the arrest of ex-footballer O. J. Simpson on murder charges. Gretzky, meanwhile, is unfailingly polite to both fans and reporters. He comes across as the guy next door, albeit a very famous one—an enthusiastic family man who honours his parents, his team and his small-town values. Amazingly enough, associates say, the image is accurate—Gretzky really is all those things.

But for sponsors, the most intoxicating ingredient in the Gretzky mix is the amount of attention he generates. Even in a year when his team would not make the playoffs, Gretzky was still featured on the news each night as he neared and finally surpassed Howe's goal-scoring record. As a result, his

The Gretzky Portfolio

These are the companies that pay to have No. 99 on their team:

Air Canada
Bradford Exchange (*collectible plates*)
Campbell Soup Co.
Chicagoland processing (*coins and medallions*)
Coca-Cola
Costacos Bros. (*personality posters*)
Domino's Pizza
Easton Sports (*hockey sticks and equipment*)
First Team Sports (*Ultra-Wheels in-line skates*)
Harleybrands (*clothing*)
L.A. Gear (*shoes and clothes*)
Sharp Electronics
The Official All-Star Café (*U.S. restaurant chain*)
Time Warner Interactive (*video games*)

Upper Deck (*trading cards*)
Upper Deck Authenticated (*memorabilia*)
Wayne Gretzky's Iceland (*ice rinks*)
Wayne Gretzky's Restaurant
Wayne Gretzky's Roller Hockey Centers (*roller hockey rinks*)
Zurich Insurance

▶ Gretzky appeared with his father in this ad for Coca-Cola.

renown extends well beyond the narrow confines of the hard-core hockey crowd. He is frequently invited on talk shows and hosted NBC's *Saturday Night Live.* His presence at a Coca-Cola-sponsored kids' hockey camp in Anaheim, California, attracted a camera crew from *Entertainment Tonight*, the weeknight half-hour of Hollywood Lite. He is no longer a mere athlete, he is a full-blown celebrity. Sharp, the Japanese electronics firm, made Gretzky the spokesman for its most important consumer product, the Viewcam—without even identifying him as a hockey player in its TV ads.

For Gretzky, kids' hockey camp is strictly business, one of many corporate obligations on his off-season slate. Companies pay him six- and seven-figure annual fees to be their spokesman, and two of the five days he works for Coca-Cola each year are spent playing host to the kids at the Future Stars camp. Gretzky's duties vary with the company. With some, he meets with staff or speaks at sales meetings. Most use him in print and TV advertising. Others simply ask him to join key clients for a day on the golf course.

—*Maclean's*, December 5, 1994

See also Video 3, Excerpts 25 & 26.

**See also
page 30.**

1. a) Why is Gretzky the ideal public relations spokesperson? What benefits does he bring to a company?

b) How do you think an athlete's corporate sponsorship agreements affect his or her reputation with fans? Explain your answer in your media log, using examples from the article or from the careers of other athletes.

2. a) Form a small group and assume you are a public relations team for a specific corporation. Brainstorm a list of celebrities who might have applied for the role of company spokesperson.

b) Write a letter of acceptance to one celebrity from your list explaining how his or her image would benefit your company.

c) Write a letter of rejection to another celebrity from your list explaining why his or her image is undesirable. Suggest five ways to improve his or her image in order to attract public relations contracts.

Public Relations Faces a Crisis

When a crisis causes public anger, fear, or blame, there are three common ways for a business or institution to respond.

Stonewall Deny that a crisis exists, refuse media questions, and resist the involvement of any outside agency. Manipulate the media by causing a drought of information. If all goes well, no information will leak to the press and the incident will be forgotten. However, if a leak occurs, which frequently happens, this response can damage your image severely. It suggests that your organization doesn't care about the public or the crisis.

Manage the News There are two ways to manage the news. The first is to delay the release of information and to share only partial, favourable, or inaccurate information with the media. The second is to flood the media with information, all carefully selected and written to make your organization look good. However, if any of the negative information you have withheld slips out, you will be accused of attempting a cover-up and will lose credibility.

Open Communication With no delays, keep the media fully informed of the facts and provide background information to put the facts into perspective. This may be embarrassing at first, but it is much less harmful than allowing rumours to surface or than being accused of a cover-up. However, some executives and company lawyers fear that admitting fault might leave a company open to being sued for damages.

The Tylenol Crisis

In the early 1980s, seven people died from cyanide poisoning found in Tylenol capsules. Fear spread across North America and sales of all Tylenol products fell sharply. Marketing experts advised Johnson & Johnson, the producers of Tylenol, to cut its losses and scrap the product. Even though Johnson & Johnson were not responsible for the poisoning, marketing experts were sure that Tylenol as a brand name was dead. But Johnson & Johnson chose to use the following public relations approach to solve the problem.

1. Johnson & Johnson launched an intensive public relations news campaign telling people what had happened and how to return the capsules. This campaign also allowed them to communicate favourable and reassuring information. They made sure that the public had easy access to accurate and up-to-date information. As a result, the company was seen to be open and concerned about helping the public.

2. Consumers were encouraged to exchange their Tylenol capsules for safe Tylenol tablets, so that they would continue to use a Tylenol product.

3. When it was discovered that the cyanide had been injected after the capsules were in stores and that Johnson & Johnson was not to blame, the company designed a tamper-resistant container and held a 90-minute, 30-city video press conference to demonstrate its effectiveness. Former users were encouraged to call a toll-free number and request a free bottle of Tylenol in the new packaging.

4. 50 million capsules were distributed to doctors for free distribution to patients.

—adapted from *Public Relations: Strategies and Tactics*
by Dennis Wilcox, 1992

**See also
Resource Binder
page 51.**

Activities

1. Which of the public relations responses described on pages 100 and 101 did Johnson & Johnson use? Why would the company choose this response? Which of the four steps in the public relations campaign do you think were most effective?

2. With a small group, plan your own public relations campaign to handle one of the possible school crises described below. Your goal is to handle the crisis, restore a good school image, and make sure your school has public support now and in the future.
   • Your school ranked lowest in a province-wide literacy test. Parents and business leaders are outraged.
   • Sporting events have been plagued by fan violence and the School Board has threatened to cancel further games.
   • After a fatal drunk driving accident involving students leaving a school dance, your community is demanding tighter control over school functions.

   Review the responses described on pages 100 and 101, then develop a plan for your whole public relations campaign. Prepare at least one public relations product or hold one event that would be included in your campaign. Several public relations events are included on page 93 and sample products appear on pages 93 and 94.

Chapter Summary

We live in a consumer society. Most Canadian jobs are involved with some stage of producing, promoting, or selling consumer products. To maintain our current standard of living, people must continue to buy things like soft drinks, designer jeans, and expensive running shoes. Advertising drives our consumer society by showing people what goods and services are available and where to find them. But advertisers are very good at using emotional appeals to suggest that consumer products can fulfill our personal needs and desires. We must ask ourselves whether advertising merely helps us meet our needs, or whether it creates those needs for us.

Corporate sponsorships and public relations campaigns bring advertising techniques into more areas of our lives, raising further ethical questions. For example, if corporate sponsors become part of the school system, how much influence will they have over how teachers teach and what students learn? Can the public trust messages from corporations and governments when they are delivered by public relations experts whose goals are to show the good side of any story?

Summary Activities

Codes and Conventions

1. Collect at least ten print ads and television commercials designed to sell products to young consumers.

a) Identify and comment on the codes and conventions used to portray youth culture and rate the ads according to how well they do so.

b) Write a short news story on the following topic: How advertisers meet or fail to meet the challenge of portraying youth culture.

Ideology and Values

2. a) The following "myths," or accepted ideas and beliefs, are basic to a consumer society:

- "New" means "better."
- Consumer goods will make you happy.
- Using the right products will make you a romantic success.

Find two or three good examples of each of these three myths in television commercials and print ads and explain how the myths are used. What do these myths, and the ads that use them, suggest is important in our society?

b) Select one of these myths and videotape or role-play a 30-second ad based on it. You might choose to parody the myth.

Industry

3. In a group or as a class, hold a debate on one of the following ethical questions related to the advertising industry.

- Should advertisers use psychographics to classify people?
- Should there be limits on how advertisers appeal to people's emotions?
- Should advertisers be free to use controversial images?

Phone or write to an advertising firm and ask if someone there would be willing to respond to the question you have chosen. If not, search through back copies of *Advertising Age* or *Marketing Magazine* in your public library to find an industry point of view on your chosen question. Use your findings as a starting point for your debate.

Audience

4. With a group, collect 25 to 50 print ads from a cross-section of magazines. Include lifestyle magazines like *Flare*, *Cosmopolitan*, *GQ*, *Harrowsmith Country Life*, *Ebony*, music and pop culture magazines like *Shift*, *Spin*, and *Rolling Stone*, sports magazines like *Ski Canada* and *Hoop*, and mass circulation magazines like *Maclean's* and *Time*. Classify the ads according to their target audiences and identify the common elements used to appeal to each audience. Choose one target audience and design an ad for an ordinary consumer product, such as toothpaste or shampoo, using the elements you have identified.

For Further Study

5. Debate the following: Resolved that corporate connections with our classrooms yield more benefits than drawbacks for education.

6. Write a short essay in response to the following statement: "Advertising shapes our values even when it does not greatly affect our buying habits." Feel free to agree or disagree with the statement.

7. Find some copies of *Adbusters*, a Vancouver-based magazine about advertising and public relations, and examine some of their satiric versions of ads. Three of these have been reprinted on pages 49 and 111. Then create some similar ads based on your most or least favourite campaign.

Chapter Expectations: In this chapter you will learn about

- how constructed environments like shopping malls and fast-food restaurants affect your lifestyle and values
- the relationship between the mass media and the constructed environments that surround you
- how television and other media create their own environments
- the issues raised by media representations of nature

CHAPTER 4

Our Constructed Worlds: Media Environments

media environments: *separate worlds that the media are able to create through repetitive messages, carefully designed settings, and stock characters, in predictable formats*

constructed reality: *a version of reality created by the mass media*

The media can create or construct a number of alternative worlds or environments. Think of the unique world that greets you as you enter a shopping mall, fast-food restaurant, or theme park. Even television can be seen as an environment, presenting to us a particular view of the world.

These environments are often linked to each other. If there is a bargain at the mall, you will probably learn about it first on television.

Television has become so central to our lives that we often take it for granted. It offers us a world of mini-environments we can step into and out of. Television has even managed to create a different natural world from the one we see on a walk or on a camping trip.

Thanks to sophisticated editing techniques and sound effects, television is able to present nature shows that are really "constructed reality."

In this chapter, you will be challenged to investigate some of the different environments and constructed realities the media create. You are invited to explore television, theme parks, fast-food restaurants, and the media's portrayal of environmental issues.

Key Concepts

Codes and Conventions

Our physical environments—houses, office buildings, shopping malls, and even theme parks—reveal our concerns for practicality, variety, and conformity. Shopping malls and theme parks, for example, are often modeled on pleasant, traditional, and idealized notions of what main street should look like. While wandering through a mall, you may notice typical codes for communicating messages—logos, store layouts, and display areas. On television, you will find codes and conventions for different genres such as news, sitcoms, police dramas, and soap operas.

Ideology and Values

The environments created by fast-food restaurants and shopping malls are designed to accommodate both the fast pace of our times and our need for instant satisfaction. In our consumer-driven culture, material goods promise emotional fulfillment, self-esteem, and happiness. Most of these products are familiar to us from their promotion on television, a media environment that some see as a mirror reflecting the desires, fears, and aspirations of society.

Industry

Large corporations dominate the retail business, and most malls feature the same stores and fast-food outlets owned by these conglomerates. With familiar logos and recognizable product lines, these retailers attract and encourage repeat sales. On television, an emphasis on commercials introduces and reinforces these familiar logos and product lines. Marketers make sure that what we see on television is available to us at the mall, and that what we see in the mall is also seen on TV. It is up to television producers, then, to provide attractive programming for audiences and for advertisers looking for exposure for their products.

Audience

Different groups want different things from media environments. Teens, for example, might just like to "hang out" at the mall, whereas adults usually shop for specific items. To effectively package environments and products, marketers must know these habits and needs. In the world of television, each of us brings different experiences and biases to viewing—after seeing a story about Greenpeace, some may perceive the group to be rebellious and a nuisance, while others may see it as heroic, saving the world from eco-destruction.

▶ How does television influence the environment of the average North American home? Has that influence changed since TV was first introduced?

Fast-Food Restaurants, Shopping Malls, and Theme Parks

Fast-food restaurants and shopping malls are constructed spaces strongly influenced by the media. Because these environments are very familiar, we may not consider examining them closely. When we do study them, however, we may discover that complex design and marketing strategies have been applied to their development. These constructions cater to people's needs and reveal characteristics of our popular culture.

When examining constructed environments like fast-food restaurants or shopping malls, consider the following questions:

- How would you describe the design of the physical space?

- How would you describe the atmosphere created as a result of the design and decor?

- What messages and values are promoted in this space?

- How do people use the space? How do they interact?

Fast-Food Restaurants

Fast-food restaurants are a familiar part of our landscape today. Statistics tell us that the majority of North American families eat in them at least once a week. Fast-food chains, in general, and McDonald's, in particular, are the essence of the American success story, and their influence can now be seen in Europe and Asia.

What makes these fast-food restaurants so appealing? John Giles, the national director for public relations at McDonald's says: "We offer people more than just fast food. It's an experience."

At McDonald's, elaborate television advertising campaigns suggest an experience of "food, folks, and fun." Commercial images show teenagers with their friends, families with small children enjoying the playground and the "treat of week," and seniors coming in with their friends because they "deserve a break today."

Wendy's has built its image on the owner and founder, Dave Thomas. Dave is shown trooping around the world dreaming up new burger combinations, or just sitting in one of his restaurants reading letters from Wendy's customers. Wendy's is presented as a place with a down-to-earth atmosphere, good food, and good value, all thanks to the friendly, fatherly character of Dave Thomas.

Harvey's makes a hamburger "a beautiful thing" because they'll make it just the way you want it. By offering choices, Harvey's has created an environment where you feel like an individual—your hamburger is made just for you—although you are participating in an experience shared by many.

According to Dr. Conrad Kottack, a University of Michigan professor of anthropology, there are elements of the fast-food restaurant that can explain its broad appeal. He claims that "McDonald's, for example, has become a virtual religious experience for millions of Americans." Regardless of where you go, "With only minor variations, the menu is located in the same place, contains the same items and has the same prices." These features are true of most fast-food chains. According to the professor, "We know what we're going to see, what we are going to say, what will be said to us and what we will eat. From that first request for a Big Mac to the final 'Have a nice day!', every move is ritualized much like a religious service."

Like many modern creations tailored to the consumer market, fast-food restaurants try to keep the customer secure, happy, and coming back for more. Ray Kroc, the founder of McDonald's, said, "When you are in this business, you are in show business. Every day is a new show. It's like a Broadway musical—if people come out humming the tune, then the show was a success."

—adapted from *The Psychology of Fast Food Happiness* by Gregory Hall, 1983

▲ *Adbusters* pokes fun at the difference between promise and reality in fast food.

1. **a)** Identify the show business aspects of the fast-food chains you are familiar with.
b) Dr. Conrad Kottack contends that McDonald's has become almost a virtual religious experience for people. Do you agree or disagree with him? Explain.

2. In your media log, describe the following aspects of fast-food restaurants you are familiar with, then decide which aspects may be common to most fast-food restaurants. Be sure to offer specific examples to support your conclusions.
   - the layout of the restaurants
   - the atmosphere created through colour, lighting, sounds
   - the decor and furnishings of the restaurants
   - the special promotions

3. According to William Meyers in *The Image-Makers*, "Madison Avenue and McDonald's had redesigned the hamburger, but more importantly, they had transformed it from a mere sandwich into a symbol of family unity."
   a) Deconstruct television commercials for McDonald's using The Pitch on page 83 of the Resource Binder.
   b) To what extent is your experience with fast-food restaurants similar to what is portrayed in the commercials?

Critics Speak Out

While fast-food restaurants are extremely popular, they also have their critics. Contrary to many images we see on television, some people suggest that a "happy hamburger land" does not exist. Instead, some critics believe that fast-food chains have become representative of a wasteful consumer ethic that promotes over-packaging, food with questionable nutritional content, and debatable values such as "more is always better."

"The message is clear: forget all your problems (does anyone really have problems?), 'give yourself a break,' come on over to McDonald's and we'll all have a wonderful time in the great consumer society. Starvation? Waste? Responsibility? Ssh! Those are ugly words, and we wouldn't want to upset the children."

—Doug Torgerson, *Environmental Education*, 1974

After testing fast food for nutrition and taste in 1994, *Consumer Reports* noted the following:

"Although fast-food companies have promoted newer, low-fat offerings—such as grilled-chicken sandwiches, lean-beef sandwiches, and assorted salads—most people still order the items we tested for this report [burgers, fries, chicken, and fish sandwiches]. Those staples are heavy in fat, saturated fat, and other nutrients that should be limited in a prudent diet. Five of the sandwiches we tested each provide more than half the fat that a person on a 2000-calorie diet should eat in an entire day."

—*Consumer Reports*, August, 1994

Investigate these criticisms using the following activities.

Activities

1. If you or any of your classmates have ever worked at a fast-food restaurant, discuss the policies in place for quality control and waste management, including recycling.

2. a) Investigate a local fast-food restaurant to determine the nutritional quality of the food and what the restaurant is doing to be environmentally responsible.
   b) Offer three to five suggestions that you think would help the restaurant remain competitive while being environmentally responsible. Be sure to consider the restaurant's food, packaging, and advertising strategies as you develop your suggestions.

3. Assess the nutritional value of a hamburger using the Canada Food Guide. You may wish to research nutritional information supplied by several fast-food chains.

The Shopping Mall

Shopping malls, like fast-food restaurants, have become part of our landscape—there are few North American communities that do not boast at least one shopping mall. The mall is a kind of wonderland—timeless and enclosed. It is a popular place for North American teenagers to gather and has made shopping a form of entertainment. The mall may very well typify North American civilization in the late twentieth century.

As a kind of "main street suburbia," shopping malls are an ideal place to explore many of our desires and aspirations as well as to observe trends in the media and popular culture. On your next visit to a mall, consider taking along a notepad, tape recorder, or video camera to observe and record the world inside the mall. If you use a camera or tape recorder, get permission from the mall manager and the people you interview before you begin. When doing your research, consider the following:

- Note the layout of the mall—the location of the entrances, directories, greenery, fountains, benches, food areas, washrooms, and telephones. How might this layout influence people's behaviour in the mall?

- How many stores are there? What stores are next to each other? Are stores grouped in a particular way? Offer reasons for the location of stores.

- What design elements or other clues communicate to shoppers that a store is a franchise and not a local store?

- Do most stores try to appeal to a variety of customers or to a specific type of customer? How can you tell? Include examples to support your ideas.

- How do the stores reflect recent popular culture trends and advertising campaigns?

- You might interview shoppers or store clerks to get their opinions of malls. Page 99 of the Resource Binder offers tips on how to conduct interviews.

The Malling of Main Street

BY WILLIAM SEVERINI KOWINSKI

The mall is Our Town's year-round carnival, the cathedral of the postwar culture, the Garden of Eden in a box. It is a mirror held up to contemporary American dreams and a fantasy haven from American nightmares—a circus in a fallout shelter. It is the strange achievement of the American Way: a utopia fashioned by the not-quite-invisible hand of merchandising. It is our latest attempt to cure the great endemic American disease of loneliness. Malls are everywhere, and everywhere they are, they are expressive and emblematic.

Its space is special because it is *protected*. The mall banishes outside threats of disruption and distraction. No cars are allowed in the mall, no traffic, noise, or fumes. The natural world can't even intrude; there's no rain or snow, heat or cold, no seasonal changes—not even gathering clouds to cause concern. This space is protected so that people will not be distracted or feel threatened; they'll relax and open themselves to the environment, and trust it. That must be part of the reason why very little is allowed in the mall that is larger, faster, or more powerful than a person.

The mall is also *controlled space.* This essential element is clearly implied in the official definition of a shopping center that I read in a publication of the Urban Land Institute, an organization that works closely with the mall industry. The operative part of that definition is: "a group of architecturally unified commercial establishments built on a site which is planned, developed, owned and managed as an operating unit." Unity, preplanning, single and centralized management are the instruments by which the mall creates its special conditions, by which it controls the environment created by enclosure and protection.

The mall environment is itself a magic theater—trees grow out of the tiled floor! Plants flourish without sun or rain!

But even before the theatrical effects, the conditions for theater are set by design and management. For a space to be a theater, the outside rules of time and space must be banished. The mall keeps out such reference

points—not only its windowless enclosure but its very uniformity (one mall resembling another) means it could be anywhere. It is placeless. Many malls banish all sense of time by eliminating clocks, and although Greengate [Mall] has a large but unobtrusively decorative clock above center court, it neutralizes time by controlling light and sound—morning, noon, and night, they are the same. The mall doesn't allow the appearance of aging—the stores are forever new in an environment that is forever now. It is timeless.

The mall is kept squeaky clean, the stores bright, the fountains gushing, the greenery fresh—or at least those are management's goals. The effect is one of almost unreal perfection. Moreover, this continuous, flowing environment with no reference to the outside—this sense of a special world—permits a kind of unity of experience within an effortless enclosure that is something like the classical theater's unities of time, place, and action. It's all here, now. The mall concentrates the drama, suspends disbelief.

Like Disney's street, the shopping mall plans and carries out a consistent design so that the mall's street looks unified, quaint yet familiar. The mall also excludes the rougher elements of real downtowns—no dives or pool halls here—and like the Disney versions, the stores are smaller than stores on town streets.

So the resemblance goes beyond enclosure, protection, and control. It struck me that the basic image the mall delivers—what this stage was set up to be—is a simplified, cleaned-up, Disneyfied fantasy version of Main Street U.S.A.

The mall is a visual experience. It's TV that you walk around in. "People-watching" is what people do in the mall when they aren't "looking for something" to buy. The images they see in the mall are from television; and how they see and accept these images has been conditioned by watching television.

"People have gotten used to two-dimensional effects, to cardboard reality," [Ralph] Keyes [author of *We, the Lonely People*] maintained. "That's what they see on television, and they accept it."

From family sitcoms and homey westerns, to the sixty-second and thirty-second dramas of commercials, television makes the mall's relentlessly upbeat and minimalist Main Street easier to accept. For millions of urban and suburban viewers, the television image may be the only visual idea they have of small-town Main Street. For residents of real small towns, this Main Street may be equally convincing on another level: It may be what they wish their reality was, and they wish it hard enough to make it so.

Advertising uses this kind of suggestion (as opposed to suggestiveness) even more extensively, and more pointedly. TV commercials try to communicate quickly with a repertoire of visual images that suggest places and the feelings associated with them. They didn't invent all these images and associations, but through repetition they've made a virtual iconography of them. In advertising talk, the image "says" something. If you want to "say" glamour and romance, you "say" Paris, and if you want to "say" Paris with an image, you show the Eiffel Tower. The Eiffel Tower "says" Paris, which "says" all kinds of

glamorous and exciting things about the product, and what will happen to you if you buy it.

The mall shrewdly makes use of these perceptual habits created by TV. It "says" Main Street with some Disneyesque design elements and a few props. The same technique is used in theme restaurants and shops. It's relatively cheap to do, and it works great.

It occurred to me that perceptual habits learned through hours and hours of television watching may also account for something else the mall seems to manage easily: its' incongruities. The mall jumbles so many kinds of stores and services, from brokerage offices to cotton-candy stands, singles bars to interfaith chapels, that otherwise don't go together. But to a population used to seeing a bloody murder followed by a candy-bar commercial, followed by soap opera sex, a religious revival, and a public TV fund drive, nothing much would seem incongruous. Compared to what is shown in sequence on one TV channel, or what is available at any moment on many channels as the viewer switches through them, the eclecticism of the mall has to be considered mild.

The similarities of television and the mall go on and on. Both of them lull and stimulate simultaneously. Watching TV, we can be everywhere without being anywhere in particular. And basically, television and the mall are in the same business: entertainment in order to sell products. Advertisers pay for TV programs so people will watch the commercials, and the commercials themselves try to sell products by being entertaining. In the mall, product sales are also based on how attractive and entertaining the mall environment and its stores are. The mall is like three-dimensional television.

Television advertises attractive ways of life and the products associated with them in its programming, and its commercials tell little stories; the line between programs and ads is therefore often blurred. At the mall, the line between "programs" and "advertising" is almost nonexistent. The fantasy of Main Street is there to sell products. Because that's what all of this—the theater, the sets, the costumes and props—is for. The mall industry even has a name for what it's all about: They call it The Retail Drama.

—from *The Malling of America: An Inside Look at the Great Consumer Paradise*, 1985

Activities

1. Summarize the author's description of how malls resemble television and try to make some of your own parallels.

2. **a)** In your media log, consider what you enjoy about shopping malls and what you dislike.
   b) Why do you think malls are appealing to teenagers? To parents with small children? To senior citizens?

3. One writer has called shopping malls "the modern marketplace, a supposed centre of community life." However, unlike centre-town squares or downtown main streets, "malls are privately owned, but publicly used, places." Outline the differences between main streets or downtown squares and shopping malls. What are the advantages and disadvantages of each environment for the community?

See also Video 3, Excerpt 28.

Bridging the Gap—A World of Shopping and Fantasy in the West Edmonton Mall

The West Edmonton Mall is the world's largest shopping mall. It also has an amusement park called Fantasyland, a NHL-sized hockey rink, a waterpark, and theme streets like the Parisian Boulevard and the New Orleans-style Bourbon Street. Stepping into the West Edmonton Mall is like entering a fantasy world.

At the West Edmonton Mall, the shopping mall and theme park have been married to create "a unique vacation destination" where shopping is entertainment and "illusion is the soul of the mall."

► According to William Severini Kowinski, "in the mall, product sales are based on how attractive and entertaining the mall environment and its stores are." How do you think the amusement park and the stores contribute to each other's success in the West Edmonton Mall?

IT'S ALL HERE!

Welcome to West Edmonton Mall – the world's largest shopping edifice; the world's largest indoor amusement park! The only mall that is both a shopper's dream and a world of excitement. Over 800 stores and services make it paradise to shoppers around the world. Just as enticing are the authentic submarine rides, the superb 18-hole miniature golf course, the Ice Palace, the world's largest indoor waterpark and so much more. Truly a unique vacation destination.

This dazzling structure - often called the 8th Wonder of the World – spans the equivalent of 48 city blocks in the prestigious west end of the City of Edmonton (metro population over 800,000), in the Province of Alberta. Edmonton – Canada's festival city – is clean, cosmopolitan, rich in culture, renowned for professional sports, and is an all-season haven for entertainment and recreation. The city is also the gateway to the breathtaking Canadian Rockies and the rugged, fascinating North.

Activities

1. a) If you or any of your classmates have been to the West Edmonton Mall, share your experiences with the class.
b) Research articles and photographs that provide information about the design and special attractions of the West Edmonton Mall. In your opinion, what might be appealing about the mall for each of the following groups: children, teenagers, adults, and senior citizens.

2. a) What other shopping malls provide entertainment as part of the shopping experience? In your media log, describe one of these malls, offering examples to support your description.
b) Produce a videotape that recreates your experience. If you do some taping at a mall, be sure to get permission from the mall management first.

Theme Parks: An Ideal World?

Theme parks have always been popular tourist attractions. For many visitors, they represent a fantasyland—an escape from everyday life. Part of the appeal of these parks can be traced to the influence of the media. This influence can be seen in many areas, from the themes that cross over from movies, to the design of special attractions, to the cast of characters that may be taken from a children's cartoon. The space in the park is well organized, controlled, and free from any interference from the outside world. Some people say these parks promote a wholesome, ideal experience for the whole family. Walt Disney, the creator of Disneyland, once said "I don't want the public to see the world they live in while they're in the park. I want them to feel they're in another world."

Reshaping History for Tourists

BY GARY KRIST

While most people support the ideology and values promoted at theme parks, sometimes these values can be controversial when serious, historical events are packaged as tourist attractions. Some people are concerned about the consequences of blurring the line between reality and fantasy.

When you read the following article, consider this question: What impact will these constructed realities have on history and on our perceptions of historical events?

CROTON-ON-HUDSON, N.Y.—In Poland, the Wolf's Lair, the Nazis' Eastern Front command post in the Second World War, is being converted into a theme resort.

According to *Travel & Leisure* magazine, staff members are to dress in replica uniforms of the Luftwaffe and Wehrmacht, and there will be dancing nightly at "Hitler's Bunker Disco."

In Germany, a 28-year-old entrepreneur has announced plans to open an amusement park near Berlin.

His theme? East Germany under Communism.

Bartenders and chambermaids will double as mock agents of the secret police. If any visitors are overheard making comments critical of the government, they will be thrown into a fake jail.

Don't look now, but history is being reshaped into a tourist attraction.

And not just its prettier moments; nowadays, no episode of our past is too tragic, no act too appalling, no institution too shameful to escape the ingenuity of the tourism industry.

Political and racial oppression seem to be the hottest thing in travel.

This kind of chamber of commerce surrealism isn't only flourishing abroad.

Near Atlanta, Ga., Holdings Inc. is developing a "Gone With The Wind Country" theme park, complete with replicas of Tara and Twelve Oaks, horse-drawn carriages, a golf course and a full array of theme shops.

It isn't the Wolf's Lair, of course, but no one involved seems to find anything at all questionable about celebrating a way of life founded on the institution of slavery, about transforming the antebellum South into an innocuous fantasy designed for family consumption.

And now the Walt Disney Company, the virtual inventor of the theme park industry, has announced plans for its own history-qua-entertainment park near Manassas, Va.

Visitors will be able to enjoy an authentic and educational "Civil War experience," complete with Mickey and Goofy, within a few miles of the battle-field where 4,200 soldiers lost their lives.

Among other things, the exhibits will dramatize the experience of slavery. "The goal here is to make this real," says a Disney official.

Another part of the park will depict the early years of industrial capitalism.

Here, in a replica steel town called Enterprise, a roller coaster will speed through a pseudo-factory, under over-flowing vats of artificial molten metal—all, one presumes, to "make real" the harsh labor conditions that prevailed back then.

And so the brave new development plans keep piling up.

But so, too, do the troubling questions they inspire: Can we really learn anything from history when its most sobering lessons are defanged and turned into vacation amusements?

Will we eventually become morally obtuse to the shame of slavery, of political oppression, even of genocide, when such things are routinely depicted as part of a feel-good experience for the whole family?

And how do I explain to my two-year-old daughter the difference between the Third Reich and the Magic Kingdom?

—*The New York Times*, November 27, 1993

Activities

1. What is your opinion of theme parks based on historical events?
- Do you think history should be reshaped into a tourist attraction? Why or why not?
- What impact might theme parks have on our perspective of historical events?

Explain your answers fully in your media log.

2. a) Investigate one of the theme parks in this article or another one you know about. Look for information in the media about how historical issues or themes are being represented.

b) Write a letter expressing your opinion of the park based on your findings.

The World Within the Box ...Television

We live in an environment we call reality, but spend hours a day watching another environment created by television. Is this television environment a mirror image of our world or a window into fantasy and fiction?

In either case, the relationship between these two worlds is obvious in trends, fashion, expressions, and attitudes. We can see it in the first year electronics student who works hard to make the grade but secretly dreams of playing guitar in a famous rock band; or in the girl next door who wants to make the cover of a fashion magazine; or in the pizza deliverer who is madly sending in show ideas to the 1-900-Geraldo Hotline. The line between fantasy and reality is blurred as we all breathlessly await our 15 minutes of fame.

When Fonz on Happy Days *took out a library card, library registrations across America skyrocketed.*

—*Teleliteracy: Taking Television Seriously,* 1992

A parish priest was asked to say mass for someone who was dying on a soap.

—*Between the Lines,* Black Rose Books

by Bill Watterson

Calvin and Hobbes

Name That Genre!

Turning on the TV enables us to enter many different worlds, all filled with diverse characters and messages. But all TV shows follow predictable patterns and these patterns help identify the particular type or "genre" of the show. Consistent character types, settings, camera work, dialogue, and editing all help us to know whether we have tuned into a soap, a sitcom, a tabloid talk show, or a police drama. Although we may not be aware of it, these codes and conventions do influence the way we make meaning out of what we view.

Use the images here to identify the three genres. Be prepared to explain how the images reveal the pattern of that particular genre.

Genre One

Genre Two

Genre Three

➡ Who is your favourite character from one of the three genres illustrated here? Why?

➡ In your opinion, is this character realistic? Is the portrayal accurate? Explain.

Television Genres: A Closer Look

Each television genre follows its own unique set of codes and conventions. As a result, we immediately know what types of shows we are seeing, even when we channel surf. But these codes do more than establish the pattern for the next hour's entertainment—they determine what values and messages each show will contain. By looking more closely at a few television genres, the distinctiveness of these mini-worlds becomes clear. Whether we are watching a sitcom or soap, TV shows tend to reinforce what the industry calls "pro-social values." These values discourage radical change and support the status quo—or what are considered the "normal" values of mainstream culture.

In the next few pages, you'll learn about the formulas used in three television genres.

genre: a type or style of television program such as situation comedy, or drama

Situation Comedy Formula

Length: Half an hour.

Setting: Indoors; an intimate, safe, personal, warm and cozy space.

Characters: Same people each week who form a loving "family" whether it be biological, with mom, dad, and the kids, or surrogate, as in the friendship or peer groupings on *Friends* and *Seinfeld*. The characters are usually good looking and financially comfortable.

Plot: The family is threatened by confusion, or change, but there is a return to "normalcy" that happily places them right back where they started. For example, if Will on *Fresh Prince of Bel Air* finds fifty thousand dollars, he must lose it by the end of the show.

See also
Resource Binder
page 53.

Humour: Stock characters or stereotypes; mistaken identities; misunderstandings; breaking the rules; jealousy; extreme points of view.

Values: Society's pro-social values are reinforced, including respect for the traditions of the nuclear family; in a cruel world, being together is better than venturing out alone; personal desires and ambitions are only successful if expressed within the family unit.

1. Using the Situation Comedy Formula on p. 123, decide whether your favourite sitcom conforms to the pattern described. Pay particular attention to the values the show promotes.

2. **a)** Sitcom humour often develops from stock characters, otherwise known as stereotypes, such as the cute but precocious kid or the frustrated father. With a partner, brainstorm a list of as many of these stock characters as possible.
   b) Place the name or description of each of the stock character types in a hat. Working in groups, draw a few character names or descriptions from the hat and write or role-play a few lines of dialogue between the characters. If you want to increase the challenge, have another group dictate the situation in which the dialogue must take place.

The TV Family

Sitcoms can convey messages about what families are supposed to be like. These representations offer insights into family relationships, the role of adults and children, the problems confronted by families, and the way problems are solved. Like other TV genres, sitcoms are constructed and connected to the

**See also
Resource Binder
page 55.**

> "Married . . . With Children *strips the sentiment from sitcoms and lets the bile pour out. It wins its audience over by shouting, in sitcom form, that sitcoms are a lie."* —from *Honey, I'm Home!*

◄ What role does television play in your family? Does it bring people together or keep them apart?

conventions of TV. Do these representations affect our expectations of our own families? Do we learn from the problems and struggles of television families or do they just provide a welcome escape from our everyday lives? Share your opinions with classmates.

"*Roseanne* is the most realistic picture of gender, class, and family relations on television today. And that's because Roseanne herself is so consciously political, so gender- and class-conscious, in every detail of her show. Roseanne fights with sexist, overbearing bosses, lashes out at her kids because she's stressed out at work, moonlights to get them through the rough days when Dan is out of work. And if these things are funny to watch, they are also deeply revealing of social and emotional truths in the lives of women and working-class families today.

—Elayne Rapping in *Progressive*, July, 1994

"As some media critics have observed, family values are celebrated and reinforced in sitcoms. Yet Dads, if they try to exert any real authority, are held up to ridicule by wives and children, who are quicker and more modern. Dads hold on to power only by giving it up and acting in a relaxed, non-confrontational manner."

—Cam Macpherson, The Association for Media Literacy, 1994

Activities

1. In your media log, write down your definition of family. What purposes do families serve? What are the roles of its members? Suggest several different types of families.

2. Select at least two popular family sitcoms and respond to the following questions:
   a) How would you describe the types of families in the shows? Consider the roles of family members, the relationships among family members and the importance of family in the story.
   b) How do the families described in a) compare with your own definition?

3. After watching several family sitcoms, respond to the following:
   a) What types of problems are experienced by most families on

television? What types of celebrations? Are these important to most real-life families? Why or why not?

b) How do the television families deal with their problems? What would you have done in a similar situation? If you could offer advice to one or more character, what would you say?

c) Does television represent all kinds of families, like single-parent families, families with no children or many children, same-sex parented families, or families with adopted children? In your opinion, is it the media's responsibility to represent these differences?

4. Compare a Canadian television family with an American one. Does the Canadian television family have the same set of beliefs and values as the American? Make a list of the similarities and differences between the two families.

5. List and describe the codes and conventions used in most family shows. How can you tell you are watching a family show and not a documentary or news program about a real family? You may wish to revisit Codes and Conventions on page 12.

Tabloid Talk Show Formula

Length: One hour.

Setting: In a studio with a live audience, panelists, and a roving host.

Characters: A strong, charismatic, and lively host who is able to draw audience members and guests out while guiding them through an unscripted discussion. Guests may be paid to appear and tell their stories, but often accept an invitation or actually request to be on the show. "Experts" are given a brief few minutes to diagnose and prescribe remedies for troubled guests.

Content: Oddities of North American life; the world of misfits; social controversies. Solutions are offered by the end of the one-hour show but they often seem quick and superficial.

See also
Resource Binder
page 59.

Emotion: Extreme—everything from tears to rage is skillfully drawn out by the host.

Values: Although individual cases may be tragic or unjust, once they are aired on public television they may seem freakish. Through watching the values of guests, the audience is given an opportunity to clarify their own values.

Talking Trash

BY LOUISE BROWN

Savvy tabloid talk show hosts seem to have teen viewers capti-vated with their sensational explorations of the seamier side of life. Where else can teens hear adults speak so openly, particu-larly about topics like relationships and sex? The following essay confronts the popularity of talk shows with teens.

They're on the threshold of their teens, with their values at the jell-point, and for guidance, they turn to . . . Ricki Lake.

But why?

"Ricki Lake! She's the best!" came the cry from both boys and girls. "She's on from 4 to 5 and she really cares about kids our age!"

She does?

"Yeah; she's got lots of young people on, talking about relationships, about boyfriends and breaking up and stuff. She's way better than Oprah; Oprah's not for us. Ricki's for us."

▲ Ricki Lake hosts one of TV's most popular daytime talk shows.

Indeed, since its launch, this hour-long show has cornered the lucrative younger audience across the continent; the under-35s who adore its chic 26-year-old host and speedy, tabloid pace. But critics call the show a bottom-feeder for deliberately choosing sensational, dysfunctional people to talk trash about themselves and each other.

"I like the fights," pronounces a Toronto grade eight boy. Another girl admits, "Yeah, it's fun to watch them diss [insult] each other."

It's not always fun. At the taping of a 1995 *Jenny Jones Show* on "secret admirers," one man discovered that his secret admirer was another man. Three days later, police say he went to his admirer's home and shot him dead.

There was a troubling echo of this on *Ricki Lake.* The topic was "The Terrible Secret You Kept From Your Best Friend!" and five women were trotted out, one at a time, to reveal to their friend, before millions of viewers, the secret they had been keeping for fear it would ruin their friendship. Then, in an insult to therapists everywhere, they were marched backstage for two minutes of "counselling" by the ubiquitous Dr. Joyce Brothers.

Day after day, Lake, Jones, Geraldo Rivera, Jerry Springer and a growing number of other talk shows trot out the

1. View an afternoon soap opera and decide which of the following comments best applies to the show's content. Be prepared to refer to specific examples when you report your findings in an oral presentation to the class or in a written report.

"The storylines reflect the collective fears, aspirations, neuroses and nightmares of the average American."
—*Seasons*, Inter-Faith Committee on the Family, 1988

"Soaps are a wonderful fantasy because they are the only place in our culture where men pay attention to women. They're running multi-million dollar businesses but they drop everything to have a cup of coffee and listen to what women have to say."
—*The Toronto Star*, April 27, 1991

"Combining both visual and auditory stimulation, soap operas expose the relatively passive viewer to many intensely arousing experiences...the viewer can simultaneously experience the emotional roller coaster of dramatized television and remain completely safe."   —*Seasons*, Inter-Faith Committee on the Family, 1988

2. After viewing two or three episodes of a particular soap, either write an article or role-play a talk show panel interview using one of the following headlines as the basis for your piece:
- In soaps, the one truly unpardonable sin is coldness of heart.
- Soaps' appeal rests in their insatiable appetite for erotic romance.
- Soaps help you cope.
- Soaps offer the best television role models for women and men.

3. Rewrite and perform (and videotape, if possible) a section of a favourite story, novel, or film as if it were a daytime soap opera.

**See also
Resource Binder
page 114.**

4. In a small group, plan, write, and perform one scene of a pilot episode of a new soap opera set in your own school. Videotape part of the episode.

Nature and the Mass Media

probe

Nature and the mass media might seem to occupy two different worlds. But the media expose us to images of the natural world every day, in advertising, on nature shows, in magazines and tourism brochures, in cartoon animals, and in language.

What is the difference between the information we gain from watching nature on TV and what we gain from actually being out in nature? Bill McKibben, an American journalist, analyzed the content and significance of a day's worth of television and compared it to the information yielded from 24 hours of camping on a mountain top beside a pond.

"Something insidious happens when you get most of your nature through television—the 'real' nature around you, even when it's intact, begins to seem dull. As one nature show producer said, 'If we showed viewers only natural, unadulterated filmmaking, wildlife filmmakers would be out of business in a year, it's so boring.' So, instead, nature films are like the highlight clips they show on the evening sports cast, all rim-bending slam dunks and bleachers-clearing home runs and knee-crumpling knockout punches.

"...Even if you did see rare animals, and somehow managed to creep up real close, chances are it wouldn't be doing anything all that amazing. Chances are it would be lying in the sun, or perhaps grooming itself, or maybe, like the duck on the pond, swimming back and forth. A lot of animals are remarkably good at sitting still (especially when they suspect they're under surveillance), and this is something TV never captures. The nature documentaries are as absurdly action-packed as the soap operas, where a life's worth of divorce, adultery, and sudden death are crammed into a week's worth of watching—trying to understand "nature" from watching *Wild Kingdom* is as tough as trying to understand "life" from watching *Melrose Place*."

—from *The Age of Missing Information*, 1993

Are the nature shows you have seen accurate portrayals of "the wild kingdom"? How do you know? What evidence is there to suggest that the representation of the natural world might not be accurate? Explain.

Adam®　　　　　　　　by Brian Basset

Marketing Environmental Awareness

See also
**Resource Binder
page 60.**

How do you prompt people to notice environmental issues when civil wars, earthquakes, famines, and terrorist bombings compete for media time?

Unlike our ancestors who lived close to the fields, forests, and seas that supported them, most of us no longer live as close to nature. Nature has become a place we visit for vacations or picnics. For many city people, the natural world has become another entertainment location, just like a mall, a theme park, or a movie theatre.

Today, most of our knowledge of the natural world comes to us through the media, which tend to turn the environment into issues, entertaining stories, or hot news items. The media give us conflict and exciting action, but they often reduce complex problems to simple conflicts between opposing sides.

Greenpeace, with close to five million members and branches in over thirty countries, is probably the best known environmental organization in the world today. Its size and influence result from the organization having learned how to attract media attention through a policy of direct confrontation. According to official Greenpeace history, the effectiveness of this technique was discovered almost by accident in 1971.

According to a Greenpeace publication, "Greenpeace began as a small group determined to do one thing: stop a nuclear weapon from being tested off the Alaskan coast. The seven activists failed to halt the blast; in fact, their boat didn't even make it to the test zone. But the voyage created so much public awareness that one year later the U.S. government canceled further tests in the area."

The key lesson for the founders of Greenpeace was not the impact of their actual confrontations, but the public awareness that the confrontations produced. This public awareness was created by the media, which recognized good audience appeal in the imaginative protests of the environmentalists.

In the years after its founding, Greenpeace activists were highly visible, pursuing the policy they called "bearing witness." They were photographed racing their inflatable boats between whales and whaler's harpoons, blocking railroad shipments of dangerous chemicals, and organizing petitions against toxic waste dumps.

One of their most spectacular stunts involved the protest over the sealing industry in Newfoundland. In 1976, to attract media attention to what they thought was the cruel killing and skinning of baby seals, Greenpeace activists chartered helicopters to fly them out to the ice flows where the seal herds were located. As reporters from several countries recorded the scene, the activists drew X's with indelible spray paint on a number of baby seals to spoil their pelts for sealers. Other camera crews recorded the killing of seals.

These actions made front page stories and television newscasts around the world, and helped European animal rights groups organize a boycott of Canadian seal fur. Public sympathy, both in Canada and overseas, turned against the sealing industry, despite their arguments that seals were no different from other animals that were killed for their hides and fur. By using the media's appetite for stories with action and powerful images, a small organization was able to sway the opinion of tens of millions of people, and put enough pressure on the Canadian government to shut down the sealing industry.

Critics of Greenpeace argue that the organization exploits the media so successfully

▲ Greenpeace protesters confront a huge whaling ship in the ocean near Antarctica.

its opponents hardly get a chance to present their viewpoint. Newfoundlanders, for example, who were involved in the seal hunt, found that the world's media were portraying them as bloodthirsty killers—thanks to the photographs and videotape supplied by Greenpeace. Little attention was paid by any media organization to the sealer's side of the issue. The stories of the seal hunters working in a traditional East Coast industry that had flourished for generations, could not compete with colour pictures of dead seal pups. By feeding the media's appetite for emotionally charged stories, Greenpeace created a powerful dramatic conflict between cruel humans and cute, defenseless animals. As a result, public outrage was easily provoked.

▲ Fisheries Minister Brian Tobin holds up a tiny turbot at a 1995 news conference addressing illegal fishing off the East Coast of Canada.

Today, Greenpeace has turned its protest method into a slogan: "Our collective actions—in groups large and small—make so much noise that our leaders no longer hear themselves think in the same old ways."

Around the world, many other groups have adopted Greenpeace protest techniques in an attempt to get media coverage and public awareness for their causes. Even governments have learned some lessons about public sympathy. In a 1995 East Coast fishing dispute with Spain, Canada attracted considerable attention and sympathy when it arrested a Spanish trawler and called a news conference across the street from the United Nations in New York to display the trawler's illegal fishing net to the international media.

See also Video 2, Excerpt 16.

Activity

1. A large number of successful environmental organizations reject the confrontational approach of Greenpeace.

   a) Research to learn what environmental organizations are active in your area.

   b) Contact at least three organizations to find out about their goals and methods. Most organizations will agree to interviews, and some will send speakers to your class. Ask them to explain how they use the media in their work.

2. Examine your local newspaper and your favourite television news show for a one-week period. Clip out any environmental stories from the paper, and note any coverage that you see on

television. At the end of the week, prepare a report on your findings, including answers to the following questions:

a) How many stories did you find in each source? What was the subject of each one?

b) What is the ratio of newspaper stories to television stories?

c) What kind of "slant" did the media give each story? Was the story made to seem important for a particular reason, such as its effect on jobs, public health, or money?

3. Whales, baby seals, wolves, and panda bears have had their survival championed by environmental groups around the world. Contact an environmental group in your area to find out about endangered species that have little or no media profile. Choose one animal and create a poster or a radio ad to highlight its situation and promote its survival, using techniques similar to those used for better-known species.

Case Study: The Body Shop Sells Commitment With Cosmetics

The Body Shop is a very successful, British-based global corporation that operates a chain of cosmetic stores in 44 countries, including Canada. Their principal claim to fame is their highly publicized commitment to human, animal, and environmental rights. The Body Shop insists on manufacturing and selling only "environmentally responsible" products that have not been tested on animals.

What will you buy to show that you care about the environment?

Their success indicates that many individuals are prepared to support such a philosophy by changing their buying habits.

Some critics have accused The Body Shop of dishonesty since some of their products contain ingredients that have been tested on animals by others in the past. The Body Shop defends its position by arguing that it sets high standards for its suppliers and publicly supports a complete ban on animal testing in the cosmetics industry.

The Body Shop has developed its own campaigns to educate its customers about various social and environmental issues. Each store has become an information centre that provides posters and pamphlets dealing with everything from violence against women to organic gardening.

Like Greenpeace, The Body Shop operates globally, and establishes links with other orga-nizations that support its favourite causes. Like a growing number of corpo-rations today, this company believes that there are clear business benefits to a strong and well-publicized commitment to environ-mental values and social activism. As con-sumers, The Body Shop's position makes us wonder about the position of other compa-nies. Will The Body Shop's competition take the same approach?

See also page 93.

◀ The Body Shop often uses their store windows to promote social or environmental issues.

Activities

1. Research at least three companies that advertise environmentally friendly products. For each product, complete the following:
   a) Describe the product and the retail outlet that sells it.
   b) Describe the perspective on nature and the environment that the product markets.

2. Take a personal inventory of your own shopping habits, then answer the following questions in your media log:
   a) Do you look for products that haven't been tested on ani-mals? If so, which products?
   b) What, if any, products that advertise their ingredients as nat-ural, organic, biodegradable, or environmentally friendly, do you use? Why do you prefer these products?
   c) Do you shop at stores such as The Body Shop or The Nature Store? Why or why not?
   d) Do you participate in recycling programs? Why or why not?

Chapter Summary

The constructed environments of the modern world, specifically the shopping mall, fast-food restaurants, and theme parks,
are intimately connected with media promotions. Television
shows us certain lifestyles and products, and the mall sells the
products to fulfill that vision. As one media critic has said,
"Television proposes and the mall disposes." Shopping malls
and fast-food restaurants cater to the fast pace of modern living and the need for maximum convenience.

Television may not always be real, although we have come to
accept the codes and conventions of its different genres, from
news to sitcoms, as a kind of reality. The driving force behind
television is to make money: to do this, programmers must create entertainment that will both hold a viewer's attention, and
be attractive to marketers looking to expose their products.

The portrayal of nature in the media is subject to the need
for dramatic, newsworthy story lines. It is no surprise to learn
that editing and staging techniques are applied to nature shows
and to campaigns to protect the environment. As we become
aware of the strategies involved in marketing environmental
awareness, we need to understand both the environmental
issues and the skillful management of the media that occurs.

Summary Activities

Codes and Conventions

1. Prominent stores in shopping malls are well known for their distinctive features, signs, and codes. Choose several of these stores and list their identifying features. Explain the messages conveyed by these features.

Ideology and Values

2. Choose five popular television shows, then list what values you feel are conveyed by the programs. When you have finished, compare your conclusions with those of your classmates. You may wish to refer to page 14 for more information on ideology and values.

Industry

3. Every week, newspapers and television programs such as *Entertainment Tonight* report on the previous week's most-watched television shows. Find a recent list and give your opinion on why the top-five shows were so popular. Explain why you agree or disagree with the ratings.

Audience

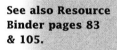

See also Resource Binder pages 83 & 105.

4. Choose your favourite ad campaign, then make a presentation outlining how effective you feel the campaign is in reaching its target market. If possible, include video, radio, magazine, and/or newspaper clips with your presentation.

For Further Study

5. For the period of one month, scan newspapers, magazines, and radio and television news programs to locate coverage of environmental stories.
a) What kind of stories got the most attention during the month?

b) Establish a set of criteria for print and TV news editors to use for accepting or declining stories, then consider the extent to which the leading environmental stories meet your criteria.

6. In groups, videotape a scene from nature. You might film animals, a sunset, a forest, or waterfalls. Edit the video, adding a sound track that will enhance the mood or action. Show it to the class, then discuss how authentic the film is. What insights did you gain that you might use when you analyze nature programs on television?

7. Imagine that you have been given $50 000 to spend, then list in your media log the items on which you would spend the money.
   a) What does your list reveal about your personal and consumer interests?
   b) What links could you make between your choices and media promotions?
   c) Are your purchases environmentally responsible? Why or why not?

8. According to Marshall McLuhan, "Environment is always invisible." What does this quote suggest about our most familiar environments such as the shopping mall or popular television shows?

9. **a)** In groups, brainstorm and list situations that might appear on a television program aimed at teenagers. Some examples might be arriving home the day a bad school report has been mailed to your parents; getting homework in all subjects the night of a basketball game; asking to borrow the car; or asking someone out on a date. Share your list with other groups.
   b) Choose one of the situations and prepare to videotape or perform it. The first time, perform the situation as it would happen in real life. The second time, perform the situation as it would happen on either a soap opera, a tabloid talk show, or a sitcom.
   c) Respond to the following two questions in your media log:
   - Which of the two roleplays was more interesting? Why?
   - It has been said that TV portrays a slice of life—but at a distorted angle. When you role-played the TV situation, how did you modify or "distort" the real-life situation to make it fit the TV genre?

**See also
Resource Binder
page 111.**

OUR CONSTRUCTED WORLDS: MEDIA ENVIRONMENTS | **139**

MESSAGE

ONDINATING

DECODED

DECIPHER

Chapter Expectations: In this chapter you will learn about

- the media images used to portray Western and developing nations
- the impact of North American media and popular culture on the cultures of other countries and regions
- the contributions of Canadian producers and performers to global media culture
- the impact of multinational corporations on the content of the mass media and on your access to the media
- how your perceptions of other countries and world events can be shaped by the media

The Global Citizen

T hanks largely to the mass media, we live in a "global village," a term coined by Canadian media guru Marshall McLuhan. This term suggests that we know a lot about each other and about what is going on in our world. But much of the information exchanged within this village arrives, like gossip, in small sound bites and short video clips, with little or no background information or explanation. The goal of this chapter is to alert you to the need to decode the media messages you receive and to recognize their biases and omissions.

Canadian media, especially television and popular music, have flourished in the global village and Canadians have enjoyed the results on their televisions and stereos. But American popular culture dominates both the Canadian and the global media marketplace, and a relatively small number of multinational media corporations control a great deal of international news gathering. To understand the information we receive, we need to understand the power and influence of the media industries, especially in news gathering and reporting. We also need to know how to judge fairness and accuracy in news reports, both in local stories and in stories about areas of the world we know little about.

global village: *the view of the world as a single interconnected community transformed by communications technology that keeps everyone everywhere informed of events and ideas*

Key Concepts

Codes and Conventions

Flashy cars, designer jeans, expensive watches and running shoes, Coke and Pepsi—the media use Western consumer goods as codes for success and "the good life." These goods suggest a wealthy lifestyle typically associated with successful North Americans.

Hungry children begging for food, violent rioters and protesters, parched and empty fields—these images all suggest poverty, helplessness, and instability. Western media usually use these as codes for life in developing nations. But neither set of codes expresses the real nature of either part of the global village.

Ideology and Values

The North American media reflect the value Western cultures place on consumerism, capitalism, individualism, and the development of advanced technologies. This ideology distorts Western media messages about less technologically and commercially developed countries. We rarely see or hear directly from the citizens of these countries, many of whom choose to retain their own culture and adapt to modern technology and commercial trends at their own pace. How, then, do we know if we are getting a true understanding of these countries and their people?

Industry

Books, newspapers, magazines, computer software, television programs, and Hollywood films are produced by a smaller number of corporations than ever before. During the 1980s and 1990s, a series of business mergers produced a small number of multinational corporations such as Disney, Time Warner and

The Thomson Corp., who control huge shares of the global marketing of entertainment and information. These multinational media corporations influence programming world-wide, help to market the stars, and often overshadow work done by locally based media.

Audience

Media producers use extensive market research to plan and design the news reports, sitcoms, and dramas we see. To a large extent we get the entertainment programs and information services we ask for. If news programs cover only wars or famines in developing countries and violence at home, it is partly because that is what audiences will watch and therefore where advertisers will pay to advertise.

◄ Fleeing ethnic violence, an estimated 250 000 Rwandans swept into Tanzania over a 24-hour period. A civil war of these proportions was news, even for the Western media. But how often did Rwanda make the news before, or after, the civil war?

Living in the Global Village

Through the mass media, people today may seem to know more about the world beyond their homes than any previous generation. But media critics warn us that people are often misinformed and misled. How does this happen?

We get a wealth of information about the world through TV news and information programs, from magazines like *Maclean's* and *National Geographic*, and from talk lines and on-line data services on the Internet. But all media are constructions. What we see, hear, and read is limited by an editor's choice of photographs, a filmmaker's vision of a country, or a writer's understanding of a conflict. We often receive these stories without background information and this leads to misinformation. As global citizens, we must learn to compensate for this information gap. To do so, we must understand how the media work and what impact they have on our understanding of the rest of the world.

"The Medium Is the Message"

BY
MARSHALL McLUHAN

In 1967, Canadian communications expert Marshall McLuhan said that the mass media were creating a "global village." The following excerpts are from his book, The Medium Is the Massage. *Despite the passage of 30 years, many of his observations are still current.*

Ours is a brand new world of all-at-once-ness. "Time" has ceased, "space" has vanished. We now live in a *global* village ... a simultaneous happening. We have had to shift our stress of attention from action to reaction. We must now know in advance the consequences of any policy or action, since the results are experienced without delay.

■ ■ ■

The medium, or process, of our time— electric technology—is reshaping and restructuring patterns of social interdependence and every aspect of our personal life. It is forcing us to reconsider and reevaluate practically every thought, every action, and every institution formerly taken for granted. Everything is changing—you, your family, your neighbourhood, your education, your job, your government, your relation to the "others." And they're changing dramatically.

■ ■ ■

Today's television children are attuned to up-to-the-minute "adult" news—inflation, rioting, war, taxes, crime, bathing beauties—and are bewildered when they enter the nineteenth-century environment that still characterizes the educational establishment where information is scarce but ordered and structured by fragmented, classified patterns, subjects, and schedules.

—from *The Medium Is the Massage* by Marshall McLuhan, 1967

Activities

1. **a)** In your own words, describe what the "global village" is.
   b) In groups, brainstorm possible answers to the following question: How do today's mass media help to maintain our electronic global village?

2. McLuhan claims that technology has forced us to rethink our ideas about family, neighbourhoods, education, jobs, government, and our relationships to others. What trends or changes in the mass media have you observed over the past five years? Do you agree with McLuhan that these trends or changes have affected your social and personal life?

See also page 190.

Global Corporations and Popular Culture

American television and films frequently show people dressed in jeans, eating hamburgers, and wearing running shoes. Thanks to satellite technology and international distribution, these media images are projected around the world. As a result, the same brand loyalties that we see here in Canada are also seen in Asia, Europe, South America, and Africa.

The global corporations that produce the jeans, hamburgers, and running shoes build factories where labour costs and taxes are lowest and buy raw materials where they are cheapest, without regard for national borders. For

"Pop culture makes the world go round, and America makes the best pop culture. By now, indeed, such products represent the largest single source of America's export earnings."

—Pico Iyer, *Harper's Magazine*, December 1991

Comparing Global Wages

Hourly wage for manufacturing workers (including benefits) in US$

1993/4

China	$0.39
Malaysia	$1.53
Thailand	$1.61
Brazil	$2.53
Mexico	$2.61
Hong Kong	$4.76
Taiwan	$5.55
Korea	$6.25
Canada	$15.69
Japan	$21.42
Switzerland	$24.84

—The World Competitiveness Report, 1995

example, Nike, the world's largest maker of sports shoes, is an American company, yet virtually all of its shoes are made in Asia. According to a Nike spokesperson, in 1993, basketball shoes made in Indonesia cost $5.60 (US) to produce, and they were sold in North America and Europe for from $73 to $135 (US). The average wage for an experienced female worker making these shoes was less than a dollar a day.

Nike then uses the difference between the cost of the shoes and their selling price to pay for multi-million dollar promotional contracts with the world's top athletes. Many other global corporations, such as Pepsi-Cola and Coca-Cola, use similar marketing strategies.

Levi Strauss, the world's largest manufacturer of blue jeans, shoots many of its international ads twice a year in Los Angeles. These ads use American pop music behind the actions of silent actors. With no language barriers, these ads can then be used anywhere Levi's are sold.

Small businesses cannot afford such attractive promotion. As a result, people all over the world may choose to buy Nikes or Levi's instead of locally produced products. With these global corporations moving into more areas of the consumer market, it becomes more and more difficult for small businesses and entrepreneurs to compete, whether they are starting a business in British Columbia, California, or India.

See also Video 2, Excerpts 17 & 19.

▶ This Moscow boy cannot afford either the model tank or the bottles of Russian-made Pepsi-Cola.

1. Select a current television or magazine ad that uses the image of a major celebrity from the world of entertainment or sports.
   - Examine and explain how the celebrity is represented in this advertisement. Is there any clue to the reason for the celebrity's fame?
   - In your media log, explain how, in your opinion, the celebrity's image affects the corporation's image or the image of any of its products.

2. Imagine that you are the marketing director of a small, new Canadian company that wants to sell its own sports shoes, hamburgers, jeans, or any popular product of your choice. You can't afford to hire any Hollywood stars or big-name athletes. How would you market your company's product to appeal to the local or national teen market? Describe two strategies in detail. Then choose one and create a print ad or audio- or videotape a commercial using the strategy. Present your ad to the class.

Canadian Content

In a global market dominated by American products and popular culture, we Canadians often have trouble seeing our own images, hearing our own music, and recognizing our own identity. American media, like American cars, are so familiar they no longer seem foreign. We grow up singing American songs, watching American shows, and following the careers of American stars. For many Canadian performers, success is measured by how well known they become in the United States.

But Canadian performers and the Canadian media excel in many areas. Let's examine two of these.

**See also
Resource Binder
page 61.**

Canadian Popular Music Booms

In the first half of the 1990s, the sales of Canadian music recordings tripled. Every type of Canadian music is still increasing its audience, as new rap, folk, and country performers emerge.

"Canadian music is experiencing, quite simply, a huge creative renaissance."

—Bernie Finkelstein, president, True North Records

See also Resource Binder page 63.

Rock bands, in particular, are experiencing a boom, and many of the best acts, such as The Tragically Hip, Cowboy Junkies, and Crash Test Dummies are earning impressive international sales. The success has spread across every region of the country, including the Far North. Susan Aglukark is one of many performers bringing regional and aboriginal music into the Canadian mainstream. In 1995, she won two Junos, one for Best New Solo Artist and one for Best Music of Aboriginal Canada.

Why the Boom?

There are two important reasons for the success of Canadian bands and independent record labels.

- Affordable technology now allows performers to make their own recordings and videos without a huge financial investment. Performers who record on their own independent labels, or "indies," rather than a major international label, have the freedom to play their own music and set their own concert and recording schedules. What they give up is the security of being managed by a powerful global corporation with American distribution channels. According to Jay Ferguson of the Halifax band Sloan: "Anybody can have a label—just put out a tape and you've got a label."

"Virtually non-existent 25 years ago, the Canadian record industry has now grown to include more than 200 record labels, along with the six foreign-owned major companies."

—*Maclean's*, March 27, 1995

- The Canadian content policies begun by the federal government in 1971 require radio stations to devote thirty percent of air time to Canadian productions. As a result, little-known Canadian bands that might never have attracted attention received exposure. When they began to write their own innovative music, audiences took note. "Canadians are no longer sucked in by look-alike, sound-alike bands. All they want to hear is music that's honest and says something to people. Fortunately, we have a lot of that right now," says Cuddy of Blue Rodeo.

1. Is there a Canadian sound? Select two Canadian performers or groups that you enjoy, and, in your media log, describe what you think is "Canadian" about their music.

2. Look over your own music collection and count how many Canadian recordings and how many American recordings you have. Do you have thirty percent Canadian content? Compare your results with a friend. Why did you buy the Canadian recordings?

Canadians in Hollywood

For millions of movie fans everywhere, Hollywood is the dream capital of the world. Its films use traditional story formulas featuring action and romance, handsome men and beautiful women, and happy endings. They set international standards for lavish costumes and sets, great cinematography, and stunning special effects.

Hollywood studios also invented the "star" system to promote their films. They transformed leading actors into celebrities who are often more famous than their films. Magazines, tabloids, and television shows keep people around the world fascinated with Hollywood gossip.

Many countries have thriving film industries of their own and there are many independent filmmakers in Canada and the United States. Although they produce high quality, entertaining films, none of them can compete with the promotional power and distribution networks of the Hollywood studios.

Hollywood films have always dominated the Canadian market. American producers and distributors consider Canada a branch of the American home market—sort of a distant northern state. As the American producer Lewis Selznik said in 1922, "If Canadian stories are worthwhile making into movies, then companies will be sent into Canada to make them."

However, since 1939, the National Film Board of Canada has been a world leader in documentary and animated films. There is probably not a single high school student in Canada who has not seen at least one NFB film. The technical excellence and creativity

| Movie Imports |
| Of all feature films imported, percentage from US |
| **1990** |

Ethiopia (1989)	69.2%
Venezuela	86.7%
Canada	63.9%
Mexico	53.0%
Hong Kong	28.9%
Japan	53.3%
France	57.3%
Germany	60.5%
Italy	67.6%
Australia (1989)	46.9%

—UNESCO Statistical Yearbook, 1994

▲ Kate Nelligan

▲ Graham Greene

▲ Gloria Reuben

of NFB productions have earned them more than 2000 international awards, including at least 60 Academy Award nominations, and, as of 1994, 10 Oscars. Well-known NFB titles include *Not a Love Story*, an anti-pornography film, and *The Big Snit* and *The Log Driver's Waltz*, both short animated films.

In 1967, the federal government created the Canadian Film Development Corporation, now called Telefilm Canada, to provide money for the Canadian feature film and television industry. By the late 1970s, Canadian filmmakers had a growing collection of successful films including *Goin' Down the Road* (1970), about two young men from Nova Scotia who move to Toronto; *Mon Oncle Antoine* (1971), a coming-of-age story of a boy in small-town Quebec; and two based on successful Canadian novels, *The Apprenticeship of Duddy Kravitz* (1974) and *Who Has Seen the Wind?* (1977).

Telefilm Canada continues to support both film and television productions. During the 1980s, Canadian film-going audiences enjoyed such successes as *The Decline of the American Empire* (1986) and *I've Heard the Mermaid Singing* (1987). In 1994, the French-Canadian film *Louis the 19th, King of the Air Waves* was a box-office success in Quebec and caught the eye of a Hollywood producer. An American production company bought the rights to adapt the script for a Hollywood movie.

On television, Canadian shows like *The Road to Avonlea*, *Due South*, and *North of 60* found loyal audiences. Canadian made-for-TV movies like *Anne of Green Gables*, *The Boys of St. Vincent*, and *Million Dollar Babies* achieved great success with audiences at home, in the United States, and abroad.

Many Canadian actors and filmmakers still go to Hollywood for steady work and the greater potential for fame and fortune. In 1995, Jim Carrey signed a $20-million (US) contract for his next film, at the time the most ever paid to an actor in Hollywood! Some of the better-known Canadians in Hollywood include directors like Norman Jewison and David Cronenberg, and actors like Christopher Plummer, Donald Sutherland, Kate Nelligan, Dan Ackroyd, Leslie Neilsen, Graham Greene, and Gloria Reuben.

Funny Canadians

Some of the funniest and most influential people in comedy, on either side of the border, are Canadians. Many of these writers, producers, and performers started out in Canadian comedy clubs like Second City and Yuk Yuk's, and spent some time on the Canadian TV comedy show, *SCTV*. Stars like John Candy, Dan Ackroyd, and Dave Thomas moved on to continued success in American TV and movies. Canadian writers and producers have also won American hearts with their work on TV shows like *Saturday Night Live*, *Seinfeld*, *Roseanne*, and *The Simpsons*, not to mention movies like *Ghostbusters* and *Wayne's World*.

▲ Leslie Neilsen

Activities

1. The phrase "a Hollywood ending" describes a happy but unrealistic ending to a movie. Choose two movies with Hollywood endings and, in your media log, explain why the endings seem unrealistic. Describe a more realistic ending for each. Read your new endings to the class and take a vote to find out which one is more popular.

2. In your media log, briefly describe a recent action-adventure or special effects movie you enjoyed and explain why you liked it. In your explanation, consider the three qualities for which Hollywood films are often praised and criticized: special effects, glamorous stars, and the portrayal of violence.

▲ Mike Myers

3. Examine the "Canadian Content" at your local video store.
   - Ask the manager if he or she knows how many Canadian films are available.
   - Find out who supplies the store with its videos. Are the distributors American- or Canadian-based companies?
   - If the video store is part of a chain operation, find out where the head office of the chain is located. If the chain is American, ask if it has any policies that differentiate the American from the Canadian outlets.
   - Write a letter to the president of the company that owns your local video store, and ask him or her how the company supports the Canadian film industry. Show a copy of the letter—and a copy of any answer you receive—to your media teacher.

4. Dave Thomas, the former head writer of *SCTV*, suggests that Canadian comedians bring "a certain 'objectivity' towards American popular culture that Americans appreciate." Watch some performances by Canadian comedians and try to explain what you think is effective about their comedy style, and in what ways it might be called "Canadian."

▲ Kathleen Robertson

The First Law of Commercial Television

BY MORRIS WOLFE

Why do many Canadians prefer American television? According to author Morris Wolfe it's because American shows have more "jolts" and a show that doesn't "jolt" its audience often enough soon loses that audience. Jolts include violent acts, rapid cutting, high decibels on the sound track, quick jokes and insults, and sudden movements—such as a character flinging open a door to enter a room.

Given the number of jolts our viewing of U.S. television has conditioned us to expect, it's easy for Canadians to fall into the trap of trying to imitate the American style. American programmers discovered some time ago that most of us have short attention spans and that those attention spans can be easily manipulated. They realized that if a long time goes by without a jolt of verbal or physical or emotional violence on the screen, or if the picture doesn't change quickly enough as a result of a jolt of rapid editing or camera movement, or movement by people or objects within the frame, or if the sound track doesn't have enough decibels, viewers will switch to a channel and programme that gives them more of those things. That's how almost all the top American shows get their audiences. They obey the First Law of Commercial Television: *Thou shalt give them enough jolts per minute (jpm's) or thou shalt lose them.*

Sesame Street is an example of a popular American programme with high jpm content. The programme, which is seen by more than 75 percent of North America's two-to-five-year-olds, became a hit as soon as it began in 1969. *Sesame Street* was unabashedly modelled on the staccato, fragmented style of a cluster of television commercials. "All art," Walter Pater wrote in the late nineteenth century, "constantly aspires toward the condition of music." In the late twentieth century, however, all television increasingly aspires to the condition of the TV commercial. *Sesame Street* consists of an average of forty-five items per hour—commercials for the letter Y, for the number 3, etc. The shortest items are five seconds long, the longest just over three minutes.

The programme is so popular that it can now be said, as it was of the old British Empire, that the sun never sets on *Sesame Street*. It's probably the most widely viewed (and celebrated) programme in the world. It's seen in almost sixty countries—in Brazil, in Indonesia, in Japan, in Pago Pago and in Zambia. Poland, Yugoslavia, and Romania show it, even mainland China has a version. The children in McLuhan's global village are all watching *Sesame Street*.

But *Sesame Street* has its detractors. Mexican writer Guillermo Tenorio, for example, has criticized *Plazo Sesamo* as

▲ Ernie stars in a typical commercial for the number 12.

an "imperialist intrusion" into the social, educational and political life of countries where it's shown. In Britain, the BBC has refused to show *Sesame Street*. The BBC's head of children's programming asked "Do we really have to import commercial hard-sell techniques into Britain because ... American children will not watch anything quiet or thoughtful?" Concern has been expressed in New Zealand about how loud and aggressive the Muppets are. Others have criticized the programme's "violence," which they see as typically American. Undesirable characters are crushed under the weight of huge objects; letters get smashed or kicked off the screen.

I spent many pleasant hours watching *Sesame Street* with my children when they were young. Now I sometimes still watch it alone. There's no doubt about the programme's entertainment value— each item is as beautifully crafted as the best-made commercials. But I do have doubts about its educational value. *Sesame Street*, after all, was originally intended to prepare children to read— to teach them "reading readiness." Research has shown that not just under-privileged children (for whom the show was originally intended) but all two-to-five-year-olds who watch *Sesame Street* know the names of the letters of the alphabet and the numbers from 1 to 20 better than those who don't watch the programme. Given *Sesame Street's* constant repetition of that information, it would be astonishing if they didn't. The result is that more children enter school these days with the alphabet more firmly fixed in their heads than ever before.

But knowing the alphabet doesn't make one literate, any more than knowing the names of tools makes one a carpenter. I find it hard to believe that *Sesame Street* prepares children to read. Books, after all, have static printed pages and a very slow pace. *Sesame Street* has neither. I would argue that what the programme teaches is not a love of books, but a love of high jpm television. One doesn't graduate from *Sesame Street* to reading Victorian novels. On the contrary, I suspect one graduates to watching high jpm programmes like... rock videos.

None of what I've said is meant to suggest that high jpm television programmes impair viewer intelligence. What I am suggesting is that a steady diet of nothing *but* high jpm television tends to condition viewers' nervous systems to respond only to a certain kind of stimulation. Their boredom thresholds are frequently so low that TV viewers find it difficult to enjoy anything that isn't fast-paced.

I have other reservations about *Sesame Street*, especially about some

of the invisible lessons it teaches. The programme is sexist; 75 percent of the cartoon and Muppet characters are male. Other invisible lessons include the notion that learning is an activity grown-ups initiate and control and that children are passive participants in; that one never goes off on tangents; and—now that stores everywhere carry a stock of *Sesame Street* products—that everyone has something to sell.

—from *Jolts: The TV Wasteland and the Canadian Oasis*, 1985

See also page 56.

Activities

1. Watch a popular American drama or sitcom and in your media log record the number of jolts per minute (jpm's) in a five-minute segment. Now do the same with a Canadian show that falls into the same category. Is there a difference in jpm's? Describe the different types of jolts that each show presents.

2. Morris Wolfe argues that *Sesame Street* does not prepare children to read books. Give reasons why you agree or disagree with his reasoning. Compare *Sesame Street* to a Canadian children's show and note how each show handles what are called "reading readiness activities" such as storytelling and alphabet recognition. Present your findings to the class.

3. The author says that children graduate from *Sesame Street* to other high jpm television programs. Survey some children in the early years of elementary school and find out what they are watching and why. Make a list of the most popular shows with this age group and calculate the jpm's on these shows. How do the jpm's on these shows compare to *Sesame Street*'s? Report your findings to the class.

Reporting the News

Thirty Seconds of News

probe

Television Bureau of Canada research indicates that seventy-five percent of Canadians rely on television news for information about their world. Yet the average TV news story is no more than 30 seconds in length, making in-depth analysis of real issues impossible.

"Television news is basically a headline service that provides you with the basic minimum of information that you need. I would hate to think that anyone is relying just on television news."
—Howard Bernstein, Director of News and Information Programming, Global News

Do you or your family watch TV news? If you want to find out about something in the news, why might you choose TV news over a newspaper or a radio report?

See also
Resource Binder
page 66.

CATHY   by Cathy Guisewite

I WATCHED THE MORNING NEWS, THE NOON NEWS, THE EVENING NEWS AND THE LATE-NIGHT NEWS.

I SAW THE LOCAL NEWS, THE NATIONAL NEWS, AND THE WORLD NEWS.

I WATCHED "NEWS BRIEF", "NEWS BREAK", "NEWS UPDATE", "NEWS CLOSE-UP", "NEWS WRAP-UP", "NEWS HIGHLIGHTS", "NEWS ANALYSIS" AND "NEWS REVIEW".

WHY DON'T I KNOW WHAT'S GOING ON ?!

Why Does News Coverage Differ?

The news media have opened the world for us. No matter where we live, we can watch events as they happen almost anywhere. But the news media also construct the world for us—selecting what we see, hear, and read about. Each newspaper and radio or

TV station reports only part of what happens on any day. If you read more than one paper or watch more than one TV station, you will see differences in the news presented.

In the news industry, there are people who function as "gatekeepers." They select the news we see and hear. **Editors** choose which stories will be covered by whom. **Reporters** decide which details to include in the stories they are assigned. **Photo and film editors** choose the few visuals to be used from the many that are shot. North American editors tend to be white, middle class, and male. Their personal perspectives often influence their choices about what is news and what is not.

See also Video 4, Excerpt 34.

The following factors guide editors as they decide which issues or events are newsworthy:

Timeliness News is transmitted very quickly today and stories quickly give way to new events. The issue or event must be current, or the story must contain new information about it.

Proximity How close to home is this news item? We are often more interested in stories that happen on our doorstep.

Prominence We are more likely to pay attention to news about world leaders and celebrities we recognize than to news about people we do not know. We are also often interested in local people, even if they are not famous.

Consequence We are also more interested in news about items that affect us directly, for example, a tax increase, a heat wave, or a series of crimes in our neighbourhood.

Human Interest Touching or funny stories that deal with our basic needs—clothing, food, shelter, affection—will always interest us. Some of the more predictable players in these stories include children, animals, or long-lost relatives finally reunited.

Activities

See also Resource Binder page 69.

1. a) In a group, take a section of a daily newspaper (the front section, or sports or entertainment sections, for example) and make a list of the headlines that appear on its front page. Set this aside for later reference. Then clip your entire section into individual articles, eliminating the ads. Shuffle them so it is no longer clear which stories were on the front page.

b) Exchange your set of articles with those of another group. From your new set, select the eight items you would put on the front page. Compare your choices to the list of original headlines. What can you tell about the bias of your group and of the original editor?

Visual News

The popularity of television news has added a sixth factor to the elements of a good news story: it must be visual. Newspapers and magazines use photographs, but visuals are even more essential in a TV newscast.

Audiences demand visual images because they add interest to a story and make it easier to understand. So when editors must choose between a story with a visual and a story without a visual, they will usually choose the story with a visual. Disasters, demonstrations, and public appearances by politicians and celebrities provide good visuals.

Visuals also seem to make a story easier to believe—after all, a photograph cannot lie, can it? But two photographs of the same event can tell very different stories. While Mohawk warriors occupied a golf course outside of Oka, Quebec, these photographs appeared on the same day on the front page of two daily newspapers. Each conveyed a distinctly different message about the event and attracted a different type of audience. Which paper do you think you would have chosen?

See also page 184.

▲ Little Watchers: Mohawk children cling for reassurance as they watch a confrontation yesterday between angry adults and soldiers at Oka, Quebec. The soldiers later retreated.

▲ A Mohawk woman pushes a soldier into barbed wire surrounding the Warriors' position at Oka yesterday.

1. Select a specific newspaper or magazine and imagine you were the editor during the Oka crisis. Which photo would you have used and which would you have rejected? Explain your choice, considering the audience of your publication.

2. Select a controversial issue at your school and take at least two photographs that express opposing points of view. Explain how the photographs could influence perceptions of the issue.

Disaster Pornography

The demand for visuals can lead to unbalanced reporting of world events. Since visuals make "good" news, and disasters provide "good" visuals, some media critics have noticed a trend toward "disaster pornography." The following description of Western media coverage of a conflict in Somalia provides an example of this kind of reporting:

> "Somali doctors and nurses have expressed shock at the conduct of film crews in hospitals. They rush through crowded corridors, leaping over stretchers, dashing to film the agony before it passes. They hold bedside vigils to record the moment of death. When the Italian film actress Sophia Loren visited Somalia, the paparazzi trampled on children as they scrambled to film her feeding a little girl— three times. This is disaster pornography."
>
> —*Media & Values*, Winter 1993

**See also
Resource Binder
page 71.**

Although disaster pornography is common in the coverage of developing countries, it also appears in coverage of events closer to home. Less dramatic stories, with less visual interest, are usually cut or buried late in a broadcast or publication.

1. **a)** In your own words, define "disaster pornography." Do either of the photographs included here fit your definition? How do you feel about the use of disaster pornography in reporting the news?
b) What advice would you give to a news crew about what they should or should not photograph when reporting on a disaster?

▲ (above) A father holds his two daughters after a three-car accident in Edmonton.

▶ (right) Actress Audrey Hepburn, a goodwill ambassador for UNICEF, visited Mogadishu to raise awareness of Somalia's plight.

2. The caption that runs beneath a photograph affects the way in which we interpret the image. Rewrite each of the captions for the photographs reproduced on pages 157 and 159. See how dramatically you can change the meaning of the photo.

3. Examine the photographs on pages 157 and 159. Choose one and use A Guide to Deconstructing a Visual on page 105 of the Resource Binder to help you explain how it is constructed. What message does the photograph convey? How could you change that message by cropping the photograph?

Spiked!
News from Developing Nations

BY VANESSA BAIRD

The idea of the "global village" suggests that through the media we all have the chance to get to know one another. But so far, Western ownership of media networks has ensured that we hear few stories from developing nations, and when we do, the people who live there rarely get to tell the stories themselves.

Good hard news combines novelty and drama within a limited timescale. Ideal events are natural or political catastrophes such as aircrashes, earthquakes, cyclones, famines and coups.

When the Third World does break into the rich world's consciousness it is usually with one of these events. As a result Western perceptions of Africa, Asia and Latin America as zones of chaos and

▲ Two women learn to operate computers in preparation for new jobs in Somalia.

misery are often exaggerated. Peter Adamson, co-founder of *New Internationalist*, regularly gives 16- and 17-year-olds and their teachers a questionnaire asking them what percentage of the world's children are "visibly malnourished." The usual answer is 50-70 percent. The true answer is one to two percent.

One reason positive stories don't get told is because they tend to unfold slowly, undramatically. Increasing female literacy in a state in Bangladesh can't compete with a flood, although the links between a mother's education and her children's chances of survival are direct and proven and the number of lives saved by educating women is likely to far exceed lives lost in a flood.

Positive stories also tend to show people quietly getting on with development. But the mainstream Western media is hooked on narratives about its own people going out and saving the world. It's a form of collective narcissism that actually obstructs vision: you can-

not see through mirrors. It's also inherently racist.

Dominant Technology

A handful of huge media empires, such as Time Warner and Rupert Murdoch's News Corp., is rapidly gaining control of every conceivable communications means and outlet—from old-established independent newspapers to Hollywood studios to cable, satellite and telephone companies.

Journalist and academic Ben Bagdikian has vividly outlined the ideal scenario for today's media mogul, whereby a magazine article generates a TV series, a movie screenplay, a sound track, a hit single, cable re-runs and worldwide distribution of videocassettes. All the companies and players involved are, of course, owned by the mogul.

At a time when some developing countries, like Brazil, India, Korea and Uruguay are becoming prolific media and news producers, there might be a real chance of realizing the 1970s dream of reversing the North-South flow of information. But, in the wake of the recent GATT free-trade agreements, the technology-rich Western media empires have *carte blanche* to flood and dominate world markets as never before.

Windows Not Mirrors

The media are too important for us to permit this concentration of power. A practical step would be to extend and apply anti-monopoly legislation or trust laws to restrict ownership. One news medium per owner would free up the market and the media to be more imaginative and more receptive to news from different perspectives—from the South, from women, from indigenous groups.

It may also allow more diverse forms of journalism to flourish. When you come down to it, any communicator worth his or her salt should be able to make us feel for another person's situation, whoever and wherever they are. The best medium of communication remains, not the fibre-optic cable, but the common thread of humanity. The moving, insightful and at times subjective work of some women war correspondents—such as Maggie O'Kane's eyewitness accounts from Bosnia for *The Guardian*—demonstrates the positive value of human-response journalism and of a fresh approach.

If, however, the media moguls have their way we are likely to end up with news from distant places and about other peoples only as an offshoot of commercial advertising.

It already happens. For the past 20 years the gradual genocide of the Buddhist Jumma people by Muslim Bangladeshi Government forces had been ignored in the mainstream media. Then, suddenly, in January 1994, the plight of the Jummas hit the news. Why? Hollywood star Richard Gere, himself a Buddhist, made a special plea for them while opening the winter sales at Harrods, London's most prestigious store.

It's good that he cares. But are we only going to hear such stories as part of another story about a famous shop and a Western celebrity who is, broadly speaking, "a local man"?

Perhaps it's time for the dominant countries of the world and their media to junk the need to have reflections of themselves, their prowess and their preoccupations in all they see. That way we might end up with a media that is closer to what it has often grandly claimed to be—a window on the world.

—New Internationalist, June 1994

Activities

1. Note your responses to the following questions:
a) Why do some places or events fail to make the news?
b) What kinds of stories about developing nations do make the news and what is often the focus of these stories?
c) What effect does typical news coverage have on Western perceptions of developing nations?

See also
**Resource Binder
page 86.**

**See also
Resource Binder
page 65.**

d) What kinds of stories about developing nations are missing from mainstream Western media coverage?

2. Investigate the presentation of news stories about other countries, particularly developing nations. Who or what is the central focus of the stories? How often is a Western person or celebrity involved? To what extent are Western business and political concerns highlighted?

3. Hold a class debate based on one of the following statements:
- The news acts as a window on the world.
- The news acts as a mirror of ourselves.

Support your responses with several examples from the news media today.

Manufacturing Consent: A Case Study of the Gulf War

Chronicle of the Gulf War

1990
August 2: Iraqi army invades Kuwait.
August 7: King Fahd "invites" U.S. forces into Saudi Arabia.
November 29: UN Security Council passes Resolution 678 authorizing use of "all necessary means" unless Iraq withdraws from Kuwait by January 15.

1991
January 16: Air bombardment launched.
February 23: U.S. launches ground war and announces press blackout.
February 25: Saddam Hussein announces pull-out from Kuwait.
February 26: Iraq says it will accept any terms.
February 27: President Bush announces end of hostilities at midnight.

—*New Internationalist*, October 1992

In 1990, Saddam Hussein, the president of Iraq, sent his army to occupy Kuwait, territory he claimed belonged to Iraq. In 1991, a UN coalition lead by the United States fought the Gulf War to free Kuwait from foreign occupation. This war provides an excellent example of how even democratic governments can use the news media to "manufacture consent," or promote their image, alter public opinion, and direct people's actions. Governments do this to win popular support for actions or ideas that might otherwise be opposed by the public. Manufacturing consent requires the careful construction and management of published and broadcast information. The main goal is to "demonize" the enemy, or opposition, so that the public feels good

> **demonize:** *to describe a person or group as completely evil, deserving of no sympathy or understanding*

about disagreeing or fighting with them. Although war provides obvious examples of this technique, manufacturing consent is also used in many other situations. As you read this case study, we challenge you to look for these techniques at work in the media today in the coverage of national or international events.

Lies or Disinformation

The most obvious way to manufacture consent is to publish lies or disinformation about the enemy. It is often impossible to detect disinformation unless someone close to the story reveals the truth. But, by then, the public might have formed opinions and taken actions based on lies.

> **disinformation:** *false information deliberately spread in order to influence public opinion*

For example, before the Gulf War, a story circulated that Iraqi soldiers had broken into hospitals in Kuwait and removed babies from incubators, leaving them to die. The story generated so much public anger that the U.S. government won support for the war against Iraq. But the story was false. It had been prepared by a public relations firm for their clients, Citizens for a Free Kuwait. If you had supported the war because of this story, how would you have felt when you learned the truth?

See also Resource Binder page 51.

Selected Images

The news media can direct public opinion by the simple selection or rejection of a photograph. Examine these images and captions and consider what impact they would have had on public support for the Gulf War. Then imagine what decisions the editor of an anti-war publication might have made. Would these photographs have been published? If so, what sort of caption would have been included? Use A Guide to Deconstructing a Visual on page 105 of the Resource Binder to assist you.

▶ (right) A Canadian corporal guards the airbase as a U.S. F-16 returns from a bombing mission.

▶ (left) An American soldier cries after learning of the death of a fellow soldier in the Gulf War.

Propaganda

propaganda: *ideas, information, or rumours spread deliberately to help a cause or to damage an opposing cause*

Propaganda is similar to a smear campaign, except the messages are often hidden in supposedly objective news stories. Propaganda makes people proud of "our" side and fear and distrust the "other" side. The Vocabulary of War chart illustrates how simple word choice can affect public opinion on an issue. The words refer to similar types of things, but the language used for our side suggests moral justice and "rightness," while the language used for the other side suggests evil motives and insane actions.

The Vocabulary of War

Our Side	Other Side
defensive	aggressive
liberation	invasion
patriotic	fanatical
hero	madman
sortie	bombing raid
collateral damage	civilian deaths
pre-emptive strike	terrorist attack
suppress a target	destroy a target

The following three steps will help you to identify and decode propaganda messages:

1. Interpret the intent. Who will gain if the message is accepted?

2. Measure the importance of the story. Is the story presented as very important or as of only minor importance?

3. Decode the text. Does the report favour one view over another?

For more information, see A Practical Guide for the Detection of Bias in the Media on page 90 of the Resource Binder.

DOONESBURY   by **Garry Trudeau**

Censorship

Censorship is used to keep information away from the public. Of the hundreds of journalists sent to cover the Gulf War, only five percent were included in the press pools who were allowed by the the American military to observe events in the war zone. Journalists from several magazines that were critical of the war were excluded entirely from these press pools. Military officials gave all stories a security review and often edited out text they didn't like. For example, the censors once changed the phrase "giddy pilots" to "proud pilots." All other journalists had to rely on reports from the pools and official press conferences for information on the war.

> **censorship:** *the practice of removing from publications and broadcasts information that may be considered harmful to the interests of those in power*

Omission

Another way to manufacture consent is to leave out all or part of a story. Sometimes this is as simple as using an incomplete quotation. For example, look at how the meaning of the following quotation changes depending on how much of it is included.

"Hussein has threatened to destroy the Coalition army."

"Hussein has threatened to destroy the Coalition army, if the U.S. crosses the Iraqi border."

Two stories omitted during the Gulf War were an interview between Saddam Hussein and Jesse Jackson, an American politician and civil rights activist, and some high quality satellite photographs that questioned the alleged size of the Iraqi force. Neither of these stories were picked up by the mainstream media.

Another type of omission is to quote only one source. During the Gulf War, the media received most of its information directly from the U.S. military and government. As news budgets are cut, journalists often have neither the time nor the resources to track down alternative views. They may have no choice but to rely on one "official" source.

See also Video 4, Excerpt 31.

The news media has great power to direct and shape public opinion. To be sure that the ideas and opinions you hold are really your own, you need to be skeptical of the news you see and hear.

1. If you wanted to show the positive side of your school, what images would you select? If you wanted to show the negative side, what images would you select? Create a photo essay or a video essay about either the virtues or vices of your school.

2. Imagine you are preparing a campaign in support of one of the following:
   - to raise or lower the drinking age
   - to shorten the school year

   Whose opinions would you want to silence? Whose opinions would you want to promote? Identify two or three interest groups such as students, parents, teachers, politicians, new drivers, or non-drinkers. List several points each interest group might make, then decide which points you would use and which you would avoid in your campaign.

3. With a small group, use The Vocabulary of War on page 164 as a model to help you brainstorm a similar vocabulary list for school life, or the environment, or a topic of your choice. Here are some examples.

Vocabulary of School Life

opportunity for improvement	failure
fire drill	recess

Vocabulary of the Environment

pesticide	crop protection
toxic waste dump	non-organic waste disposal site

You might then use your vocabulary list to write a propaganda-style story about your topic.

4. Interview someone on a controversial topic, then use the interview as part of a videotaped or printed news story about the topic. Using one or more of the techniques for manufacturing consent described in this chapter, edit what the person said to distort the original intention. Describe the decisions you made. Is this practice ethical? Explain.

**See also
Resource Binder
page 87.**

Chapter Summary

In many ways, the mass media have made us global citizens. They provide entertainment and information for millions of people. The media help construct our understanding of our own country and even of our own communities, as well as our impressions of areas of the world we may never visit in person. But the mass media are dominated by American media products and they often present an American perspective on the world.

Despite competition from south of the border, we have created space for our own media images and messages. Canada has developed a very successful music industry, and Canadian television and films are respected the world over. Our challenge as Canadians is to maintain our unique media presence and to promote it in the global marketplace.

The news media bring to our attention issues that might otherwise seem too remote to concern us. Our nightly news is full of political, social, economic, and ecological stories that link Canada to the rest of the world. But the information in these reports, especially on television, is always limited and can be misleading. The coverage of the Gulf War is only one example of this problem. Our challenge as global citizens is to become well informed and to evaluate responsibly all of the information we receive.

Summary Activities

Codes and Conventions

1. What are some of the stereotypical codes and conventions associated with one particular type of music such as rap, hard rock, or new country? Create a CD cover or plan and tape a short music video (one verse or one chorus of a song) in which you avoid or spoof these stereotypes.

Ideology and Values

2. Many magazines and newspapers carry ads seeking aid for poor people in developing nations. What messages do these ads convey about developing nations, their citizens, and their relationships with industrialized nations such as Canada? To what extent are these messages accurate representations of life in developing nations?

Industry

3. Contact a local radio station and interview an on-air personality or producer about how Canadian content regulations have affected the Canadian music industry and Canadian radio stations. Prepare a report of your interview and draw your own conclusions about whether or not the content regulations are a good idea.

Audience

4. Use the front page of a daily newspaper or a list of the stories from an evening news broadcast and predict how each member of your family would respond to the stories covered.
  • Which stories would they watch or read?
  • Which images would catch their attention?
Based on your predictions, which member of your family most closely fits the "audience profile" the newspaper editor or news broadcaster has in mind?

For Further Study

5. View one network's evening coverage of foreign news. List the stories and the visuals that accompanied them, and record your responses to both. How much information did the commentary provide on the causes and background of each story? What questions were left unanswered? How did the television medium itself limit the coverage?

6. As a class, select an ongoing news story and compare how it is covered by several news media. You might choose to follow the coverage of a war, a natural disaster, a human rights issue, or a similar topic. Some of your classmates should read daily newspapers; others should read magazines, including some that are not a part of the mainstream (for example, *The Nation*, *Canadian Forum*, *New Internationalist*); and others should watch American and Canadian television news coverage. Compare how the different media cover the story, using some of the insights and skills you have learned in this chapter. Summarize your findings as a class.

7. Contact people in your school or community who have traveled extensively or who have lived part of their lives outside North America. Interview them about the impact American popular culture has had on the countries they know. What do they think are the advantages and disadvantages of having easy access to American popular culture? The Student Handout on page 99 of the Resource Binder offers tips on interviewing. Record your interviews and create an edited two- to three-minute sound collage of the most interesting comments.

Chapter Expectations: In this chapter you will learn about

- how new and traditional technologies are converging to create a new multimedia environment
- the limitations, dangers, and strengths of communications technology
- how new artistic achievements are possible for those working creatively in the media
- the possible impact of new and converging technologies on education

CHAPTER 6

New and Converging Technologies

New communications technologies are profoundly transforming our world. From interactive video conferencing for businesses to multimedia home computers, changes are everywhere. Living in an information culture is exciting yet stressful: we must deal with huge quantities of information and we face an abundance of entertainment options.

This chapter challenges you to investigate the personal and social consequences of our information- and technology-rich world. Technology offers enormous creative potential for those who have access to it. But it also threatens people with the possibility of loss of privacy, of addiction to video games and the Internet, and of a widening gap between those who have access to technology and those who do not. What will happen to people who cannot afford the latest technologies? What kind of education or career choices will be available to them? And finally, perhaps the most important question we face is: Will we be masters or servants of the new technologies?

Key Concepts

Codes and Conventions

Because there are so many different kinds of technologies, from CD-ROMs to video to phone-faxes, each with its own code, there is no single unifying set of codes. Instead there is a constantly shifting and evolving language of communication. The convergence of technologies such as computers, television, and telephones is resulting in a new, integrated environment, known as "multimedia."

Ideology and Values

People welcome new technologies that give them a competitive edge in business or provide new sources of entertainment. However, today's technology goes out of date quickly and many people are obsessed with owning the newest and trendiest electronic toys. Should we be concerned by this trend? Or by other technological trends, such as the more realistic "win-or-die" action video games, or manipulated video images, or the possibilities for electronic invasion of privacy?

Industry

Media conglomerates such as Disney and Time Warner are buying and integrating film, video, publishing, and computer companies, and telephone services. As a small group of global conglomerates gains control of almost ninety percent of the communications industry, people will find their media and communications choices limited. Whether watching a film, phoning a friend, or reading a magazine, chances are the medium of communication you choose will be controlled by one of only a few corporations. This control may give these corporations excessive social and political power and technological influence.

Audience

For those who have access to them, new technologies offer tremendous opportunities for learning and entertainment. Films, music, even school, may all be transformed by new technologies. But are all these changes for the better? For example, the Internet provides virtual communities for people with interests ranging from up-to-date scientific information to the latest gossip about a television show. But most communication on the Internet is anonymous: participants need not identify their race, their gender, their age, or their education. Users must carefully evaluate the information they receive. And critics worry that much of the activity on the Internet is a waste of time and takes people away from real-life encounters with other people.

▶ New technologies change the way we tell our stories. What might a child learn from this high-tech fairy tale?

Music: An Electronic Culture

Over the past few decades, young people from all economic and cultural groups have, as one writer said, "seized the most advanced forms of modern technology to present their experiences and aspirations to a wider world."

Two of these forms of modern technology are music sampling and music videos.

Play It Again: Music Sampling

When you hear new songs on the radio these days, do they sometimes have a familiar ring? If you listen more closely, you may discover that in many cases you did hear that sound before. It may be a James Brown beat now used in a rapper's groove, or a recycled '60s riff reappearing in a current dance-floor hit. These oldies' echoes are the result of a high-tech sound technique, known as digital sampling. It was first used in the late '70s, when an enterprising disco DJ played a short sound bite from an old record over and over again to give it a funky new spin.

> "Sampling has made it possible for people who are not trained in conventional musical skills to bring musical ideas together in new and expressive ways."
>
> —Jim Aiken, *Keyboard Magazine*, 1994

The technique took a quantum leap forward when the first electronic samplers were introduced around 1980. Unlike synthesizers, which generate sounds artificially, samplers record real sounds. Anything audible is eligible: pre-recorded music, drumbeats, human voices, even ordinary noises like a slamming door. Samplers transform these sounds into digital codes, which in turn can be manipulated to produce melodies, rhythm tracks, and complicated webs of sounds. Today, sampling

> "Playing trumpet is an expressive and creative act. Playing a trumpet sample is just playing something that somebody else did."
>
> —Bob Moog, father of the synthesizer, *Keyboard Magazine*, February 1995

has become an accepted technique for both alternative and mainstream recording artists. For example, Madonna used Public Enemy's rhythm track for her hit "Justify My Love" and Vanilla Ice used David Bowie's "Under Pressure" for his hit "Ice Ice Baby."

Some musicians believe music sampling is a creative tool that adds excitement to the music industry. One musician had this to say about sampling: "It's a really fascinating way of seeing what someone is going to do with your music. It's amazing. I send out the raw materials and it comes back a new song." Other musicians believe sampling is "theft, pure and simple."

See also
Resource Binder
page 72.

Activities

1. What is your personal opinion of the union of music and technology that we hear in sampled and synthesized music? Note your responses in your media log, then with a group debate the following: Sampling undermines the creative imagination.

2. **a)** Create your own collage or soundscape of sampled sounds and play it for your classmates. How different is this new form of sound recording from traditional composition? Consider the sounds produced and the emotional appeal.
   b) Where do you see the future of music going—back to the basics of "unplugged" acoustic sounds, or forward into technologically produced music? Explain your opinion, referring to your experience in a) above.

3. Can electronically produced music be judged by the same criteria as traditional music? Develop a five-point guide to evaluating the artistic merit of sampled music.

See also
Resource Binder
page 91.

Music Videos Evolve

Although music videos are no longer new, the technology used to produce them is still evolving. Early music videos were used primarily to promote recordings and performers. Since videos were very expensive to produce, only a few already successful performers used them. Today, videos still promote the sale of tapes and CDs, but as Denise Donlon, MuchMusic's director of music programming, says: "the technology is

"I like the idea of a song having a visual image as well. It gives it another life almost, a different face."
—Shania Twain, *TV Guide*, October 14, 1995

now available to anyone who knows how to use a camcorder." Now all musicians, top-40 or alternative, can use music videos to promote their music and their experiences.

"There are certain bands that can't deliver on the live side or that rely so much on video that perhaps they take away the mystique of the band...you may get bigger faster, but you also fall faster."

—Jake Gold, manager of the Tragically Hip, in the *Toronto Star*, Wednesday, September 28, 1994

Video technology has changed dramatically since music videos first achieved mass-market success in the early 1980s. The following brief out-takes from *Rolling Stone's* "The 100 Top Music Videos" follow the move from hand-drawn animation to computer "morphing" in just seven years.

1984: The video for "You Might Think" by the Cars, co-directed by Jeff Stein and Charlex, was the first of its kind to elaborately manipulate blue-screen technology. Periscopes coming out of bathtubs, the band playing on a bar of soap and Ocasek's face transposed onto the likeness of a fly are just a few ways that "You Might Think" brought animation into the video world.

1985: For the MTV award-winning video "Take On Me" by a-ha, Mike Patterson "had to draw from between 12 to 17 drawings a second, so with two or three minutes of animation, that's...a lot of drawing."
1991: In "Black and White" by Michael Jackson, "the series of morphing faces as the song fades is indeed extraordinary."
—adapted from *Rolling Stone*, October 14, 1993

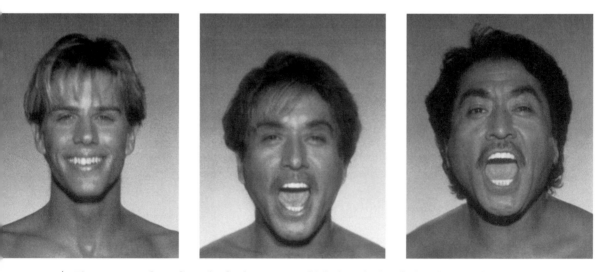

▲ These are two faces from the final sequence of "Black and White," plus the morphed image that appeared between them.

1. How have changes in video and audio technology changed music videos? Compare a music video from the eighties with a current one, looking at the use of
   - techniques such as camera angles, lighting, and editing
   - technologies such as animation and special effects
   - issues raised by the videos
   Prepare your comparison in the form of a review.

**See also pages
30 & 32.**

2. Technological and artistic changes have brought videos a long way from their relatively simple beginnings. In a small group, form your own Video Awards Committee and develop at least five criteria you would use to judge the artistic merits of videos.

3. Create your own mini music video for one verse or a chorus from one of your favourite songs. Be as technologically and artistically innovative as your equipment will allow.

Digital Wizardry in Hollywood

Today, computer-generated imagery and special effects are revolutionizing Hollywood. At a fraction of what it costs to make a regular movie, directors are working with images on a computer screen as often as they work with actors on a set. The possibilities today seem endless: images of actors can be electronically "pasted" into unfinished scenes, whole scenes can be electronically "stitched" into a film sequence, and new images can be invented or "sculpted," all using computer software. While some critics worry that movies will become too technical, others believe that the technology opens up a new world for filmmakers and audiences alike. "In Digital Hollywood you simply won't be able to trust your eyes—and you won't care, because entertainment will be taken to a higher level."

> "The coming of digital movie production is upon us. It has been compared to every major event in film history, from the introduction of color to the invention of the medium itself."
>
> —Laurence Hooper, *Rolling Stone*, August 11, 1994

"First the silents. Then the talkies. Now, the digitals."

The room is chilled for the comfort of machines, and it hums with their heartbeats. Racks of computers stand in rows, linked by cables and patchcords, small panels displaying each processor's performance. Outside, programmers work in front of large screens, harnessing the digital horsepower. This could be the electronic brains of a nuclear power-station or the nerve centre of a telephone network. Instead, it is a converted conference room in the Los Angeles headquarters of Sony Pictures. This is the high-tech face of moviemaking today.

It is also the new face of TV and video production and multimedia gamemaking as well. To make three dolphins swim up a flooded street in a Guns n' Roses music video, a 3–D image of a

▲ Digital wizardry placed these dolphins in a city street, without disturbing the dolphins.

dolphin was sculpted inside a computer, replicated digitally, flooded with a simulated image of seawater—and then the whole thing was electronically stitched into a video sequence of a rainy street scene.

To insiders, such feats of digital wizardry seem anything but miraculous. In fact the job looks quite dull: somebody sits in front of a computer, sketching stick figures or writing program code. To the public at large, the result can be a startlingly realistic herd of stampeding dinosaurs in Steven Spielberg's blockbuster movie *Jurassic Park*, or the fantasy world of multimedia computer games such as TIE Fighter or Doom II.

Sometimes, on the other hand, the digital scenery looks wholly unremarkable—no more than a landscape backdrop, say. Such inconspicuously realistic images are, in their own way, just as amazing as Mr. Spielberg's bounding dinosaurs. They too can be solely the figment of a computer's silicon brain. William Birrell, a Sony executive, calls the use of digital effects to create normal-looking images that would be too difficult or expensive to create otherwise "synthetic reality." Like the digital sampling used for recording music on a CD, digital production techniques in film "let you sample reality and use it for your story," says Mr. Birrell. The great advantage—in video as well as audio—is that what has been done need not be obvious.

Nor need it be done merely to satisfy a director's creative urge. When Brandon Lee died during the shooting of *The Crow*, the movie was salvaged by electronically pasting digitized images of the actor into unfinished scenes. To save money, the director making *In the Line of Fire* inserted a digital sequence of Clint Eastwood (playing a secret-service agent trying to protect the president) into old newsreel footage of a George Bush motorcade.

Hollywood's enthusiasm for digital techniques is also a response to the fascination of the movie-going public. A film that pushes the limits of technology can be a draw for that reason alone. Effects may be patently false; done well, they are still marvellous to watch. In recent films, such as *The Mask*, the digital effects shared top billing with the stars. The ability to do new things with digits suggested a movie that could not otherwise have been made. There are many such examples.

From the pioneering work of Disney's *Tron* and George Lucas's *Star Wars* in the 1970s to the liquid imagery of *Terminator 2* in 1991, computer effects have allowed film directors to explore the furthest reaches of their imaginations. They have frequently broken box-office records in the process. From *E.T.* to *Jurassic Park*, seven of the ten biggest-grossing movies ever made have been "effects" films.

Now digital techniques promise to cut the cost of making movies as well— and not just for blockbuster science-fiction epics. Within a few years, it seems, movies using state-of-the-art digital techniques such as *True Lies* (made for a reputed $120m) will cost

The Top Ten All-Time Domestic Grossers

1. *E.T.—The Extra-Terrestrial*
2. *Jurassic Park*
3. *Star Wars*
4. *Home Alone*
5. *Forrest Gump*
6. *The Lion King*
7. *Return of the Jedi*
8. *Jaws*
9. *Batman*
10. *Raiders of the Lost Ark*

—*Variety Magazine*, October 1994

only half as much to produce. No wonder the digital studio business is booming. At a conference on digital production in Los Angeles, speakers reckoned the new industry was growing at 25-50% a year. The new digital studios scattered around Los Angeles are about to bail out the old Hollywood system.

And just in time, too. Over the past five years Hollywood has seen American cinema audiences decline by a further 10% while its costs have soared 66% in money terms—more than twice the rate of inflation. The average "negative cost" (i.e., the cost of producing a finished negative, before print-making, advertising and marketing) of a movie made by a Hollywood studio is now $31m. To that has to be added $29m to cover the average amount the industry spends per film on print-making ($2m), marketing ($14m) and advertising ($13m).

What has all this to do with the digital studios that are flourishing in the New Hollywood between Santa Monica and Marina del Rey? One thing: digital technology will transform the economics of movie-making. In two main ways, it will mean lower costs and bigger profits.

First, the computer breaks the stranglehold that the unions have over staffing on a production set. Instead of using teams of carpenters, decorators and electricians (not to mention focus pullers, best boys and gaffers) to build and light sets, entire scenes can be synthesized inside a computer and then "composited" digitally with live-action shots of the actors playing their roles against a blue screen. That is how Warner Brothers made *Interview with a Vampire*.

Second, the computer can render the movie star irrelevant. Top stars such as Mel Gibson demand anything up to 15% of a movie's gross, which can be as much as $20m. Kevin Costner's asking price is a straight $12m. Rather than pay even a fraction of such fees, leading video game designers have started to develop "virtual actors" that have

▲ Digital monsters like this T-rex from *Jurassic Park* offer filmmakers tremendous freedom for telling stories.

"Digital artistry will allow actors to bioengineer themselves, or be bully bioengineered, to perfection. A performer with no aptitude for dance, for example, can have all the right moves programmed in. Stars will be constructed from the choicest body parts."

—Paula Parisi in *Wired* magazine, December 1995

personalities and attitudes all of their own. And if virtual images of a herd of dinosaurs can be created inside a computer and made to stampede across a movie screen, why not synthesize the human actors digitally as well?

While launching *Jurassic Park*, Universal Studios also introduced its new sound system, Digital Theater Systems (DTS). With DTS, sound is contained on a CD-ROM disc, not just on the 35mm film itself. As many as six tracks of crisp, thunderous John Williams' score and a variety of dinosaur snorts (frequency response: 20 hertz to 20 kilohertz) are precisely cued to the CD player by a digital time code printed on the film. A traditional analog sound track is programmed to cut in should DTS cut out. The combination of digital imaging and digital sound is so convincing and so terrifying that *Jurassic Park* has been put off limits to many children.

Today, nothing seems out of bounds. "We may even see," says Ross, "a film starring Arnold Schwarzenegger and the digitally recreated version of Marilyn Monroe."

George Lucas maintains that digital technology will ultimately strengthen filmmakers' ability to tell stories—

"especially the ones that are easy to write but hard to film, like those involving dinosaurs." The technology "is also about doing period action dramas for less money. In one sense, if you can cut costs, you can tell more stories."

After the dust of digital revolution has cleared, however, most of Hollywood's traditional tricks and processes will be left on the cutting room floor. The way films are planned, shot, edited, composited, and shown to an increasingly discerning public will fall to those who handle pixels [square electronic dots] best.

Already, a crowd of lean and hungry pixel pickers are primed to put their CGI [computer-generated imagery] skills to work. What does getting started entail? "All you need is about a million dollars," says David Brown, president of Blue Sky Productions, a prize-winning computer-generated animation company in Ossining, N.Y. "Start with a $48,000 Silicon Graphics Iris Extreme setup and some $47,000 Softimage software; create a network of other computers and software; add a staff of CGI artists and programmers."

Veteran filmmakers, meanwhile, will have access to tools that were unavailable until recently. George Lucas is planning another *Star Wars* trilogy; does that mean the droids will be digitally created this time? "Yoda maybe, but not the droids," he says. (Yoda was performed by puppeteer Frank Oz.) Asked whether filmmakers will eventually eliminate actors and replace them with automated images, Lucas admits it's possible, but points out that a crucial element would be missing: "the quirkiness" that only a human being can bring to a role.

Michael J. McAlister, visual effects supervisor of Industrial Light and Magic and author of *The Language of Visual Effects* (Lone Eagle Publishing), says, "What's missing today is computer people who are also filmmakers. The next generation will belong to the person who wants to make movies but also studies computers. Digital technology will reach from previsualizing scenes to SFX [special effects] to restoring old films—and much more."

While all this is taking shape, SFX pioneer Douglas Trumbull (*2001: A Space Odyssey, E.T.*) is sequestered in a rural nook of western Massachusetts. He recently showed a visitor through his own digital world where he's creating ride-film experiences for special venues such as theme parks and hotels. At one point, he

See also Video 4, Excerpt 36.

stopped at a pen-and-ink storyboard tacked to a wall. It was an outline, he explained, for a digital work-in-progress: three action theater "entertainments" for the Luxor Hotel in Las Vegas, where audiences will move and sway as they are immersed in a world of images. To Trumbull, this represents the future of entertainment: intensely interactive film experiences and simulated rides.

"Movies," Trumbull says with utter conviction, "are dinosaurs."

Watch out. There's a bunch of raptors out there who would disagree.

—adapted from "Computers Come to Tinseltown," *The Economist*, December 24, 1994 and "The Wow Factor" by Peter Britton, *Popular Science*, November 1993

See also
Resource Binder
page 77.

1. **a)** Describe the advantages and disadvantages of digital technology for the movie industry.

   b) Identify and debate at least one ethical question raised by the use of digital technology, for example, "bringing back" dead actors, inventing digital actors, or using a digital version of a living actor.

2. **a)** Do an "image scan" of one of the special effects movies mentioned in the article. Select two or more powerful scenes or images and explain what makes them memorable. Consider elements such as setting, character, performance, action, sound track, and special effects.

   b) How do the images or scenes you have identified affect the meaning or impact of the movie?

3. Write a review of your most favourite or least favourite special effects movie. In the review, comment on how the high-tech special effects affected the story being told.

See also
Resource Binder
page 101.

4. Have you ever had a ride-film experience? If so, describe it in your media log. Do you think that these events will replace movies? Why or why not?

5. Many animated and special effects movies generate huge sales of related merchandise such as T-shirts, stuffed animals, and action figures. Visit a local department or video store to investigate the marketing of movie-related merchandise. If possible, ask the store manager about the schedule for promoting the merchandise and how that schedule relates to the movie and video release dates.

The Animated Steve Williams

BY DEIRDRE KELLY

Steve Williams is a Toronto-born animator who recently brought fame to our land with an Academy Award nomination for special effects in *The Mask*. Williams, who went to L.A. a couple of years after graduating in 1986 from Sheridan College in Oakville, Ont., works at George Lucas's Industrial Light and Magic. In addition to the dazzling work he produced in *The Mask* and *Jurassic Park*, Williams also threw his mental weight into *Terminator 2: Judgement Day*, *The Abyss*, and *The Hunt for Red October*.

Sharp, intelligent, oozing self-confidence, Williams is also aware of his role in a rapidly expanding industry. He's pretty well at the top of his field. And he claims to hate himself for it. He says in the seven years he has been with Lucas's operation he has seen it grow from a staff of six to today's staff of about 400. Almost 20 percent of the company is made up of Canadians, most of whom Williams has personally placed. "I feel really bad," he deadpans. "I've hired 70 Canadians for ILM. I guess it's good for them, but it's bad for Canada because so much of the talent is leaving the country."

He appeases his guilty conscience by noting in the next breath that while Canada is one of the world leaders in animation and graphic design, it is slow to develop "home product." Williams himself might have stayed if there had been opportunities for him here. He is a proud Canadian who boasts that his father and grandfather were, like him, born and raised in Toronto. But he'll have a chance to spend more time in the city starting in the fall [of 1995], when Sheridan College makes him one of its first teaching partners in a new artist-in-residence program for the 1995-96 academic year. Williams will also continue to work in the United States; he's currently working on new animation sequences for a 20th-anniversary edition of Lucas's *Star Wars*.

—from *The Globe and Mail*, Friday, April 14, 1995

Activities

1. Write or visit Sheridan College in Oakville, Ontario to find out more about its animation technology program. In 1995, it was the only program of its kind in Canada and the biggest one in North America. Find out about the entrance requirements and the job opportunities available upon graduation. How many of those jobs are in Canada?

See also page 149.

2. Investigate the programs available in multimedia technology at two colleges or universities in Canada. Write to one of them for information or arrange a tour to learn about the facility and the programs offered.

See also Video 4, Excerpt 38.

3. Write to or interview a student, staff member, or someone working in the multimedia or animation industry to find out about the kinds of work being done now and about possible future developments.

Down to a Photo Refinish

BY KATHY SAWYER

Thanks to computer technology, images in film and photography can be easily manipulated. Critics say that the same techniques used to entertain us can also be used to deceive us. The following article explores image manipulation and reliability in the news.

Computerized image-making means one picture is worth a thousand words of warning.

In the young world of computerized image manipulation, the lion lies down with the lamb (a commercial aired during the 1994 Olympics); Marilyn Monroe flirts with Abraham Lincoln (the cover of the February 1994 *Scientific American*); and the U.S. Capitol looms behind a reporter who is miles away inside a studio (a 1994 ABC News broadcast).

Phonied photographs are nothing new. The concern is that the latest technology makes deceptions much easier and faster to accomplish and much harder—if not impossible—to detect.

In digital imaging, the elements of a picture are converted into computer language—numbers made up of zeros and ones. The image then produced is a montage of square electronic dots (pixels). By changing the numerical value of each dot—a process that leaves no "footprints"—the software can be used to alter the picture at will: matching tones and colors and blending the edges. (A similar, though much more complicated process, is used to manipulate video images, as depicted, for example, in the hit novel and movie, *Rising Sun*.)

It may be impossible to tell how a digitized image has been manipulated, except by comparing it to the original print or negative. But with the advent of cameras that take electronic photographs, many images now begin in

"By decade's end, we will look back at 1992 and wonder how a video of police beating a citizen would move Los Angeles to riot. The age of camcorder innocence will evaporate as teenage morphers routinely manipulate the most prosaic of images into vivid, convincing fictions. We will no longer trust our eyes when observing video-mediated reality."

—Paul Saffo, *Wired*, May 1993

▶ President Clinton never posed for this photograph. His face was digitally pasted onto a model's body.

digital form. There is no permanent original.

In an article in *Scientific American*, William J. Mitchell, dean of the school of architecture and planning at the Massachusetts Institute of Technology, says it is up to the image consumer to beware: "The question of how to distinguish visual fact from fiction is becoming increasingly urgent as we witness the explosive proliferation of digital-imaging technology. We are approaching the point at which most of the images that we see in our daily lives, and that form our understanding of the world, will have been digitally recorded, transmitted and processed."

In the past decade or so, media executives, photojournalists and others have been swept up in the seductions of the emerging technology—and in controversy over how to use it ethically while preserving credibility. *National Geographic* magazine moved the pyramids of Egypt closer together on its cover. Ted Turner began to colorize old movies. Humphrey Bogart and other deceased movie stars were reincarnated electronically to party with the living in television ads. *TV Guide* put talk show host Oprah Winfrey's head on actress Ann-Margret's body. When actress Helen Hayes died, the *Washington Post* published a picture of her alone on stage, after electronically erasing another actress from the scene.

Most news organizations have a policy prohibiting alteration of images that are presented as depicting reality. The difficulties arise when people try to define the wavery boundary that distinguishes news photos from those used for other purposes.

For what it's worth, Mitchell notes, the more information (detail, color, light reflections, shadows, etc.) a picture contains, the harder it is to manipulate without introducing internal inconsistencies that signal deception. But soon, analysts predict, the technology will be available for use by anyone with a home computer (with unknown implications for the old family photo album) and electronic images will fly instantaneously back and forth along the information superhighway.

Freedom of image, like freedom of speech, will be complicated.

—*Washington Post National Weekly Edition*,
February 28, 1994

Activities

1. Explain why critics are increasingly concerned about the use of image-manipulation technology. Refer to the quotation from *Wired* on page 184.

2. What kinds of changes to published or broadcast images are acceptable and what kinds are not? Should the public be informed of any alterations? Consider photographs used in the fashion and entertainment industries vs. those used in photojournalism, news, and other information sources.

**See also page
197, Activity 7.**

3. Write or visit a local newspaper, a television station, or a video production company, to learn about the ways in which computer technology is being used.

4. Role-play a conversation between a photojournalist who explains image manipulation used on a published photograph and one of the people who appeared in that photograph. Review the article here and "The Retouching Epidemic" on page 50, for ideas about what changes could have been made.

Living in Cyberspace

Personal Technology probe

media

"Technology isn't just a tool—it is inherently personal. Take a look at the way the automobile has totally changed society. With multimedia we are witnessing another fundamental change in the way we live and communicate with one another," says futurist Ruben Nelson. He believes multimedia systems will result in a drop in the demand for the services of professionals in a wide range of disciplines. Instead of dropping into the office, he says, people will increasingly turn to their computers for financial, legal, personal, and even medical advice. He also points to the school system as an area ripe for change. As government searches for ways to avoid building new schools, and parents look to maintain greater control over their children's education, multimedia systems could provide an answer.

"We still think schools and universities are places you have to go to to learn. This technology blows that concept away. If we do maintain schools in the future, it will be for the social aspects—not because we need them to teach people."

—Mel Duvall, *Calgary Herald*, November 9, 1994

See also Resource Binder pages 74 & 76.

What do you think Nelson means when he says technology is "inherently personal"? How have cars, phones, bank machines, video games, computers and the Internet affected your personal life?

Games in Cyberspace

More and more computer users, especially students, are discovering the pleasures of computer games. Below is the fictional evolution of one computer game player.

I started out playing Nintendo games when I was a kid. The Nintendo machine used its own software and hooked into my TV so I could play Super Mario Brothers and games like that. By the time I was 10 years old, I had the hand-eye coordination of a fighter pilot, but I wanted better graphics, better sound, and more excitement. So I graduated to the Video Arcades and the latest games in high-tech fantasy adventure.

I have two favourites types of games. The first are simulator games, where you work realistic controls to stay on course or find your target for combat. I can choose from driving a race car, a motorcycle, a tank or, my personal favourite, flying high in a jet.

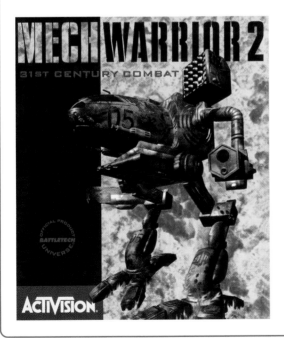

These games work just like the flight simulators used to train pilots and astronauts. I've heard that the game technology is really catching up to the realism of the genuine simulators. Would I love to try one of them!

The second type are combat games with all kinds of gruesome and dangerous situations. I lead my hero through a realistic fight to the death with lots of blood and gore. I can take my computer hero up against a whole crowd of pre-programmed enemies, or I can fight with a friend, using tandem controls. Either way, the loser dies in hideous and horrible ways.

> *"The trick is to engage the player on an emotional level and get them to really identify with and care about the characters—then you have to take the consequences for your actions, be they your death or someone else's."*
> —John Antinori, game designer, *PC Power,*
> January 1995

What I really want now is a better computer at home, one with enough speed and memory to run the newest games. They have fantastic picture and sound quality and really complex storylines. The games that run off CD-ROMs are almost like television or movies. I've seen some really terrifying horror games, ones that would scare anyone, even me! These new games even have realistic characters, people you can really get to know. They seem so real, you grow to either love 'em or hate 'em.

Activities

1. The majority of computer game buyers are young males. Why do you think this is so? What kinds of games attract female players? Do many such games exist?

2. Traditional games offer some clear benefits to their players. Chess teaches strategy and long-range planning. Monopoly teaches the basics of finance. Scrabble improves spelling and word recognition skills. What benefits do the new computer games offer their players?

3. Some people find computer games addictive. In your media log, explain the addictive features of these games and suggest how to play them without becoming addicted.

4. Game designers are using improved graphics to offer increasingly gory and realistic-looking violence. In your opinion, is this harmless escapism or a dangerous appeal to the worst side of people? Does playing violent games make the player more violent? Discuss this question with a group including at least one experienced player of violent computer games. Present your opinions to the class.

The Virtual Reality Supermarket

BY FAITH POPCORN

Trend-tracker Faith Popcorn has pointed out that people are leaving their homes less often for entertainment. Instead, they are assembling their own elaborate home entertainment centres. Popcorn calls this phenomenon "cocooning." In groups, brainstorm three lists of ideas related to "cocooning"—one in favour of it, one opposed to it, and a third labeled "interesting," for ideas that fit neither of the extremes. As a class, discuss the advantages and disadvantages of cocooning and home entertainment centres, then read the following article.

Cocooning. Safe in your own cocoon at home, you decide, at your convenience, to do your supermarketing. You don goggles and gloves, then lie back on your eiderdown comforter. You don't have to leave home, even get dressed.

In your coziest flannel nightshirt, you embark on your...

Fantasy Adventure. Imagine yourself going off to a glorious summer roadside stand to buy produce. (You can even squeeze the tomatoes—and actually feel

whether they're ripe that day, through your glove.) Point your finger toward Marrakech or Jamaica to look at the markets your spices come from. Visit a French bakery to scan the baguettes and croissants. (Who's to say "smell" won't be part of virtual reality soon?) Smile at the face of the friendliest butcher in Iowa as he shows you his best cuts of meat, before shipment to your store. (If you're really curious, take a look at the fields where the cattle graze.) See your butter and milk at the dairy, your bottled water at its pure spring beginnings. Then you'll order them with a different eye, a different attitude. Supermarket magic.

Egonomics. The "Home Reality Engine" is a smart machine, with intimate knowledge of you. If you're on a low-fat diet, it guides you to healthy shopping. It knows the ingredients you need to put into your chili recipe, and guides you down the "aisles" so you don't forget cumin, say, or beer. It knows your political bent and special concerns, and can flash updated information to you about "green" packaging or boycotts or changes in kosher certification. With virtual reality, you literally choose your own world. You get to decide what you want to be real. Could there be a greater expression of customization than that?

Down-Aging. The virtual reality supermarket is real-life Nintendo shopping for adults, the ultimate toy. Fulfill your grown-up obligations while playing a really neat game.

The Vigilante Consumer. With complete product information always available to you, you are empowered to make informed choices. Interactive programs make it possible to speak back to manufacturers, and monitor the progress of promised reforms and company track records. "Labeling" possibilities are endless—there is no longer a physical limitation to size.

Supermarkets should be thinking *now* of ways to segue into virtual reality tomorrow. This means putting capital spending into warehousing and delivery systems —not into new store designs; they'll soon be obsolete. It means becoming the *information-center* supermarket today, the supermarket known for personal service—to build a strong, believable foundation for the virtual reality supermarket it will have to become in the future.

See also Video 4, Excerpt 37.

—*The Popcorn Report*, 1992

1. **a)** How likely is it that virtual reality shopping will ever replace the mall? Explain your answer.

   b) Virtual reality shopping has been described as a "really neat game." Think of other virtual reality games that could be invented to make daily chores more fun. Present your ideas to the class.

2. What would be the advantages and disadvantages of virtual reality shopping? Would people go virtual shopping alone or with friends? Would products still need fancy packaging? How would people who were not "on-line" shop? Would there be a danger of developing virtual reality shopping addiction?

3. In your media log, describe a virtual reality shopping expedition that you would enjoy. What would you shop for? What places would you like to visit and what information would you like to be available? Share your ideas with the class.

The Technology of Learning

BY BARBARA KURSHAN
AND CECILIA LENK

The following is one vision of what the future of education might be like using new electronic communications technologies. As with most predictions for the future, it may become dated as the technologies continue to evolve. But its goal is to spark thought, discussion, and research into how new technologies should be used in education.

Technologists and futurists agree that tomorrow's classroom will be radically different from the one you're in today. But many schools already have in place some of the communications technology that will make this vision possible.

Since all students will be able to network electronically in order to "attend" class, the classroom could be anywhere and could include anyone: children, teenagers, adults, and senior citizens. They could work from their homes, schools, and offices, or even a local park or community centre.

Once on-line, students could work and share information with teams or small groups. The network would also provide multimedia links with schools, libraries, businesses, governments, and experts in any field of study. Students would have access to up-to-date information on evolving issues and rich text, graphic, and video resources. They would also be able to visit, through video teleconferences and virtual field trips, places that are too far away to visit in person.

Students will be able to share their work easily with the world beyond the classroom. Class survey and poll results could become part of the global data base. Class videos, made using high-quality video resources, would be available to anyone with access to the global network. And learners could discuss their ideas with experts working in the field they are studying, as well as with their teachers. This will be interactivity at its best.

—adapted from "Crossroads on the Information Highway," *Annual Review of Institute for Information Studies*, 1995

Activities

1. Examine the communications systems currently in place in your own school. How much of the vision described above is already a reality in your school?

2. How would attending an electronic classroom change your learning experience? Use the following questions as a framework for discussion with the class or for writing in your media log:
a) How would you feel about school and learning if you attended an electronic classroom like the one described?
b) How might working with the new technologies change your views of the world? Your sense of identity? Your career ambitions?

See also Video 4, Excerpt 40.

3. In the role of a student attending an electronic school, write five daily journal entries or tape five video-journal entries. Use the following prompts to guide your writing:
- How would attending an electronic school affect your social life?
- How would you get to know your teachers and how would you ask them for help?
- How would students not on the network fit into school life?

See also Resource Binder page 94.

Voice Recognition Turns Computing on Its Ear

BY GEOFFREY ROWAN

Many of us would like to talk to our computers, usually to ask them why something isn't working or to find a missing file. But we have to use a mouse and keyboard. Now, technology promises something much more natural: computers that can follow spoken instructions.

Science fiction writers imagined it decades ago. The computer industry tried tackling it in the early 1980s. But it's only with the arrival in 1995 of hardware that's up to the task that voice recognition technology is expected to make its breakthrough.

In the months and years to come, consumers will be given the option of using the spoken word to tell their appliances and computers what they want them to do.

The emergence of voice or speech recognition will cause wholesale changes in the way people work with computers and in the way the computer industry designs its products. That translates into the growth of an immense industry.

"The speech recognition market today could be compared to the personal computer market 20 years ago," said Alicia Smith of Lernout & Hauspie Speech Products, a Belgian company with North American headquarters in Woburn, Mass. "The potential is huge and that cannot be understated."

Industry guru William Meisel, whose Encino, California based TMA Associates publishes *The Speech Recognition Update* newsletter, says voice recognition technology already generates about $500-million (U.S.) globally in annual sales, but that's in a very narrow niche.

As voice becomes the interface of choice, he estimates the global demand for speech recognition products will

interface: *the way people and computers communicate, for example, through keyboards and monitors*

reach about $26.3-billion a year by the end of the decade, thanks to a new generation of microprocessors—the electronic brains inside computers.

"The hardware is now good enough so that voice can be used," said Isaac Raichyk, chief executive of Toronto-based Kolvox Communications Inc. "The trick is in figuring out how to use it."

—*The Globe and Mail*, March 27, 1995

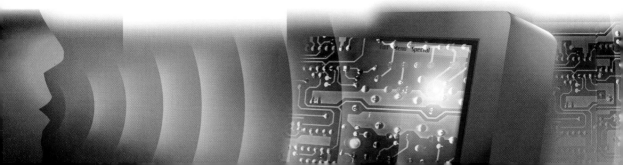

Will Your Next Computer Listen to You— and Talk Back?

As voice recognition becomes more commonly available, all kinds of things may become possible. Voice recognition technology combined with other computer and communication applications may make some of these future developments possible.

- A computer that answers questions and even makes conversation. Media stars may license their voices for electronic duplication. Your computer could sound like your favourite actor or singer.

- A computer that monitors your home entertainment and media systems and follows your voice commands. You could simply say: "I'm going to the mall. Tape *The Young and the Restless* for me if I'm not home in time."

- A computer that inputs your school assignments from your dictation and corrects your grammar and spelling. When you finish an assignment, your computer could print it out at home, or transmit it directly to your teacher's computer at school.

Activity

1. What will computers be like in the future? Develop a detailed description of the possible impact of future technology on daily life. You might write it as a news report on life in the year 2010 or audio- or videotape it as a dialogue between a person and a computer. When you have completed your description, join with a group and discuss your responses to the questions below.
   - Would a computer like the one you have described be a threat to anyone's privacy?
   - Would you be in control of such a computer or would it control you?

Privacy and Your Electronic Identity

probe

media

While you are at school, you accumulate many student records, including your marks, which are all stored on computers.

Outside of school, when you subscribe to a magazine, join a music or sports club, or send a cheque to a charity, your name and address are stored on other computers. This information may then be sold to more companies with computers, who use it to sell related products or to seek more charitable donations.

When you shop with a credit or debit card, where you shop, where you travel, and where you like to eat are recorded on yet another database. If anyone could access these computer files, they could learn almost everything about you.

How much information about you do you think already exists on computer databases? What kinds of businesses and organizations would be interested in this information about you? How might they use it?

◀ We can use digital cards like this one to access our bank accounts, to go shopping, to get special membership discounts, and to place phone calls. Someday we may be able to buy car insurance or get a loan from an automated outlet similar to today's bank machines. What advantages or disadvantages does this type of technology bring with it?

Chapter Summary

The new communications technologies affect us at all levels of our experience—personal, social, and political. On the personal and social levels, we need to question whether these technologies interfere with human relationships when they make it possible to communicate without meeting people face to face. On the political level, interactive technology gives many of us instant access to information on the issues of our times. But does this access to information really lead to improved democracy? What about all the people who do not have access?

As citizens living in a time of diminishing resources, we need to ask who benefits from these new communications technologies. Governments? Corporations? Private citizens? The powerful? The poor? Whenever possible, we must take control of this "techno" universe and tell our own stories, using the technologies available to us such as the camcorder and the Internet. Only by telling our own stories do we gain control over the representations and interpretations of our world.

Summary Activities

Codes and Conventions

See also cartoon on page 173.

1. Our culture tells its stories through the spoken and printed word, and through films and television. But the new communications technologies give us new ways to tell our stories, for example, through e-mail, Internet chat lines, bulletin boards, home pages, CD-ROMs, and home videos. How might each new technology or medium influence the form and content of our stories? Write a story or choose one that has already been told in print, film, or TV. Then adapt all or part

of the story for one of the new technologies. Describe how you had to alter the story to adapt it to the new medium. How might these changes affect the impact or message of the story?

Ideology and Values

2. Research the opinions advanced by both those in favour of, and those opposed to, violent computer games. In your research, besides looking at books and periodicals, interview at least two of the following: teachers in your school, computer and video store personnel, and parents of children who play computer games. Write up and present a report of your findings.

3. The impact of the new communications technologies on family and household routines will be considerable. In groups, evaluate the impact of current technologies on your household, and then speculate on the impact more sophisticated new technologies will have in five or ten years.

Industry

4. In a group or as a class, debate one of the following resolutions related to the high-tech communications industry:
   - All personal information stored on computer, whether it relates to shopping habits, annual income, or personal health, should be strictly private.
   - The government should develop guidelines to restrict offensive materials on the Internet.
   - Citizens should have the right to hack into government files to find out what their elected representatives are doing.

Audience

5. "Get a life!" With a group, videotape a panel discussion or talk show session on the following topic: The new entertainment and communications technologies—such as computer games and the Internet—take time away from meaningful, real-life human experiences. Be sure to include responses from a variety of audiences.

For Further Study

6. Imagine what kinds of computerized technologies will be part of the ideal home by the year 2020 and share your ideas with a partner or the class. Include ideas for entertainment, personal and financial planning, housework, and school or job-related activities The following list of current technologies should help you get started: computers, interactive television, multimedia, phones, fax machines, modems, video games, e-mail, the Internet. Write a diary or tape a video-journal entry for a typical day in the life of a teenager in 2020, highlighting the use and influence of technology. In what creative and practical ways might communications technologies affect your life?

7. With a group, try your own hand at video manipulation. Make a short videotape (max. 1 min.) of your classmates doing something active like running and jumping, or simply proceeding with their daily activities. Then use editing, background music and sound effects, and any other video manipulation you have the technology to use, to create a specific mood or effect. You might experiment with rapid editing cuts to create high "jolts per minute." Each group should present their video and explain their editing rationale. How did the editing and special effects shape the story or message of the original video?

See also page 152.

8. Reread the Media Probe: Personal Technology on page 186, then do some research into the changes that multimedia technologies have already made for professionals such as doctors, lawyers, and office workers, or for schools, colleges and universities. As you do your research, keep in mind the comment that technology is "inherently personal." How would the changes you have learned about affect the personal lives of the people involved?

index

ACKNOWLEDGEMENTS

Every reasonable effort has been made to acquire permission for copyrighted material used in this book, and to acknowledge all such indebtedness accurately. However, all errors and omissions called to our attention will be corrected in future printings.

TEXT

Bad Behaviour Can Prove Profitable by James Christie. From *The Globe and Mail*, February 13, 1995. Reprinted with permision; **Rap Expresses Young People's Anxiety and Joy** by Roger McTair. First appeared in *The Toronto Star*, January 4, 1994. Reprinted with permission of the author; **Music to Live By** by John Daly. Reprinted with permission of *Maclean's* Magazine from an article which appeared on February 22, 1993; **The Arab Stereotype: A Villain Without a Human Face** by Jack Shaheen. From *Extra!* the magazine of FAIR; **Body Obsession** by Mary Nemeth. Reprinted with permission of *Maclean's* Magazine from an article which appeared on May 2, 1994; **"Our goal is to get a variety...,"** quote from Joan Pennefather. Reprinted by permission of *Maclean's* Magazine from an article which appeared on March 29, 1995; **Gender Representation in Advertising**. Adapted from MediaWatch, *Trends in the Media Portrayal of Women*; **The Retouching Epidemic** by Marshall Blonsky. Article originally appeared in *Allure*. Reprinted by permission of Georges Borchardt, Inc. **The Taste Test** by Louise Brown. © Louise Brown, reprinted with permission from an article in *Starweek*, January 7, 1995; **TV Isn't Violent Enough** by Mike Oppenheim, M.D., reprinted with permission of the author; **How to Produce Advertising that Sells** by David Ogilvy. From OGILVY ON ADVERTISING, published by PRION (UK) and RANDOM HOUSE (USA). Reprinted with permission of Multimedia Books; **Psychographics**, from THE IMAGE MAKERS by William Meyers. Copyright © 1984 by William Meyers. Reprinted by permission of Times Books, a division of Random House, Inc.; **"If someone from another planet visited...,"** quote by Oliviero Toscani from an article by Desmond O'Grady, published in *The Toronto Star*, August 20, 1995. Reprinted with permission of Desmond O'Grady. **Educating the Market** by James Pollock, reprinted with permission of *Marketing* Magazine; **Schools Go Commercial** by Michael Jacobson and Laurie Mazur. From MARKETING MADNESS: A SURVIVAL GUIDE FOR A CONSUMER SOCIETY, published by Westview Press. Reprinted with permission of the authors; **"There is an obvious reason for business's rising interest...,"** quote by Erika Shaker from *Education Forum*, Fall 1995. Reprinted by permission of Erika Shaker; **Fake News** by David Lieberman. From *TV Guide*, Los Angeles Metropolitan Edition, February 22, 1992. Reprinted with permission; **Gretzky Inc.** by James Deacon. Reprinted with permission from *Maclean's* Magazine from an article which appeared on December 5, 1994; **Where's the Fat?** Copyright © 1994 by Consumers Union of U.S., Adapted with permission from *Consumer Reports*, August 1994. Although this material originally appeared in *Consumer Reports*, the selective adaptation and resulting conclusions presented are those of the author(s) and are not sanctioned or endorsed in any way by Consumers Union, the publisher of *Consumer Reports*; **Excerpts from THE MALLING OF AMERICA** by William Severini Kowinski. Copyright © 1985 by William Severini Kowinski. By permission of William Morrow & Co. Inc.; **Reshaping History for Tourists** (Tragedyland) by Gary Krist. From *The New York Times*, November 27, 1993, reprinted with permission from *The New York Times*; **Talking Trash** by Louise Brown. © Louise Brown, reprinted with permission from an article in *Starweek*, April 1, 1995; **"Something insidious happens...,"** quote from THE AGE OF MISSING INFORMATION by Bill McKibben. Copyright © 1992 by Bill McKibben. Reprinted by permission of Random House, Inc.; **The Medium is the Massage** by Marshall McLuhan and Quentin Fiore, produced by Jerome Agel, © by Jerome Agel; **The First Law of Commercial Television** by Morris Wolfe. From JOLTS, THE TV WASTELAND AND THE CANADIAN OASIS. Copyright © 1985, published by James Lorimer & Co. Ltd. Reprinted with permission; **"Somali doctors and nurses have expressed shock...,"** quote from 'Disaster Pornography from Somalia' by Rakiya Omaar and Alex de Waal. From *Media & Values*, Winter 1993. Copyright © Center for Media Literacy. Reprinted with permission; **Spiked! News from Developing Nations** by Vanessa Baird. Reprinted with permission from *New Internationalist* from an article which appeared in June 1994; **"The life of Africa's varied...,"** quote by Ezekiel Makunike. From *Media & Values*, Winter 1993. Copyright © Center for Media Literacy. Reprinted with permission; **"Playing a trumpet is an expressive...,"** quote by Bob Moog. © 1996 Miller Freeman, Inc. Reprinted from the February 1995 issue of *KEYBOARD* Magazine; **The Animated Steve Williams** by Deirdre Kelly. From *The Globe and Mail*, April 14, 1995. Reprinted with permission; **Down to a Photo Refinish** by Kathy Sawyer. Copyright © 1994, *The Washington Post*, Reprinted with permission; **Media Probe: Personal Technology**, quote by Mel Duvall. From *The Calgary Herald*, November 9, 1994; **Excerpts from The Top 100 Videos**, from *Rolling Stone*, October 14, 1993. By Straight Arrow Publishers. All rights reserved. Reprinted by permission; **Digital Wizardry in Hollywood**, adapted from 'The Wow Factor,' November 1993 edition of the *Los Angeles Times*, reprinted with permission of the *Los Angeles Times* Syndicate and 'Computers Come to Tinseltown,' December 24, 1995 edition of *The Economist*, reprinted with permission of *The Economist*; **The Virtual Reality Supermarket**, from THE POPCORN REPORT by Faith Popcorn. Copyright © 1991 by Faith Popcorn. Used by permission of Doubleday, a division of Bantam Doubleday Dell Publishing Group, Inc; **The Technology of Learning** by Barbara Kurshan and Cecilia Lenk. From CROSSROADS ON THE INFORMATION HIGHWAY, published by The Institute for Information Studies, 1995. Reprinted with permission; **Voice Recognition Turns Computing on Its Ear** by Geoffrey Rowan. From *The Globe and Mail*, March 27, 1995. Reprinted with permission.

PHOTOGRAPHS

p. 4 (top) CBS/Courtesy of The Everett Collection; **p. 4 (centre)** TM and © 20th Century Fox/Courtesy of The Everett Collection; **p. 4 (bottom)** Alliance Communications production; **p. 6 (top)** Alliance Communications production; **p. 6 (bottom)** Toronto Blue Jays Baseball Club; **p. 13** *Mrs. Doubtfire/Star Wars/Frankenstein:* The Everett Collection; **p. 13** *The Lion King:* © Disney Enterprises, Inc.; **p. 26** The Everett Collection; **p. 28** Reprinted with permission of Starter Canada; **p. 30** Scott Morgan/Debbie Ayrest with permission from Joop! Jeans & Bates Alliance; **p. 35** Canapress/Andrew Vaughan; **p. 36** Urban Alliance on Race Relations; **p. 37** The Everett Collection; **p. 37** Canapress/John Moore; **p. 45** © Disney Enterprises, Inc.; **p. 49 (left)** An *Adbusters* Ad Parody Vol. 3 No. 3 Winter 95; **p. 49 (right)** An *Adbusters* Ad Parody Vol. 4 No. 2 Winter 96; **p. 52** Sante D'Orazio Studio & *Allure;* **p. 60** The Everett Collection; **p. 69** SMW Advertising; **p. 73** Pepperidge Farms Canada; **p. 75** Volvo Canada; **p. 78** © 1992, McDonald's Corporation; **p. 79** McLaren McCann; **p. 80** Guess?, Inc. **p. 81** United Colors of Benetton, Concept: O. Toscani, Spring/Summer 1992; **p. 82** DIESEL Canada; **p. 84** National Eating Disorder Information Centre; **p. 85 (top)** Mount St. Vincent University; **p. 85 (bottom)** Nipissing University; **p. 93 (right)** Canapress/Elise Amendola; **p. 93 (left)** Liquor Control Board of Ontario; **p. 94** Imperial Oil Limited; **p. 99** ® registered trademarks appear courtesy of Coca-Cola Ltd. Reproduced with permission of Coca-Cola Ltd. & Wayne Gretzky's agent, Michael Barnett; **p. 109** FPG Historical/Masterfile; **p. 111** Powershift Advertising Agency *Adbusters* Vol. 3 No. 4; **p. 118** West Edmonton Mall; **p. 122** NBC/Courtesy of The Everett Collection; **p. 122** The Everett Collection; **p. 122** NBC/Courtesy of The Everett Collection; **p. 127** The Everett Collection; **p. 133** Greenpeace; **p. 134** Archive Photos; **p. 136** The Body Shop; **p. 143** Canapress; **p. 146** Canapress/Alexander Zemlianichenko; **p. 150 (top)** Great North Artists Management Inc.; **p. 150 (centre)** Gary Goddard and Associates; **p. 150 (bottom)** Baumgarten & Prophet Entertainment; **p. 151 (top)** Paradigm/PR **p. 151 (centre)** Creative Artists Agency; **p. 151 (bottom)** Noble Talent; **p. 153** Copyright © 1996 Children's Television Workshop; **p. 157 (both)** The Toronto Star Syndicate; **p. 159 (left)** Canapress/Walter Tychnowicz; **p. 159 (right)** Canapress/Hassan Amini; **p. 160** Canapress/Olga Shalygin; **p. 163 (right)** Canapress/Hans Deryk; **p. 163 (left)** Canapress/David Turnley; **p. 176** Pacific Data Imagery; **p. 178** Courtesy of Geffen Records; **p . 180** The Everett Collection; **p. 184** David Laurence; **p. 187** Activision is a registered trademark of Activision, Inc. © 1996 Activision, Inc. Reproduced with permission; **p. 194** Poulides/Thatcher/Tony Stone Images

ILLUSTRATIONS

Kevin Ghiglione: pp. 1, 106-107, 189, 191, 192-193; Paul Watson: pp. 22-23, 140-141; Bill Boyko: pp. 66-67, 170-171; Bill Frampton: cross-reference icons

---

COVER

Symbols of mass media and popular culture are in motion around an individual who is part of a world of communication, information, time, and change. These images contrast with the physical world, which is represented as constant and unchanging.
